PART 1
------> first edition <------

by Karen Lyn Davis

Coolmath.com, Inc.

Coolmath Algebra: Part 1
First Edition

© 2007 Coolmath.com, Inc.

ISBN-13: 978-0-9791628-0-0
ISBN-10: 0-9791628-0-7

All rights reserved.

No part of this book may be reproduced or publicly presented in any form, by Photostat, microfilm, xerography, projection, or any other means, or incorporated into any information retrieval system, electronic or mechanical, without the written permission of the copyright owners.

All inquiries should be addressed to:

Coolmath.com, Inc.
P.O. Box 4386
Costa Mesa, CA 92628-4386

http://www.coolmath.com

Printed in the U.S.A.

Teachers and home schooling parents, please read the next page to find out about fair use in the classroom.

Copyrights & Fair Use in the Classroom

First of all, thank you for taking the time to read this. I'm sure you're all aware of copyrights and their importance in protecting the work of the creators of unique and innovative educational materials such as Coolmath.com and Coolmath Algebra.

Fortunately, for teachers and students there is something called "fair use." Simply put, fair use is the exception that allows teachers and students to use (within some very restrictive guidelines) copyrighted materials for educational purposes in the classroom. I've found that many teachers are unaware of the specifics regarding fair use of copyrighted materials like websites. (I, too, was quite uninformed in this area until I started to do some investigating!)

For students, fair use is easy! Students can use graphics and content all they wish (without permission) as long as it is for a class assignment. The only restrictions are that the "borrowed" content cannot be displayed in a public forum such as a website without the permission of the copyright holder and the content cannot be put into a situation where it can be distributed or copied. Students cannot give the content to someone else for use... **Specifically, you cannot make copies of this book or any portion of this book for your friends.**

For teachers, it's a bit more complicated and MUCH more restricted. To cut to the chase, **the key is to never use anything that would cause the copyright owner to lose income.** For example, photocopying any portion of a textbook (or other book) for classroom use instead of buying copies of the book for each student. Or downloading or printing a portion of a website for classroom use instead of visiting the site "live" so that the publisher can receive the income from the online ads.

So, where does this put us with Coolmath Algebra? If you want to use Coolmath Algebra in the classroom, you have two options available:

1) Visit the Algebra area of Coolmath.com live in the classroom. **Coolmath.com, Inc. is granting you the right to use the WEBSITE Coolmath.com in the classroom as much as you'd like -- AS LONG AS YOU VISIT THE SITE LIVE!** You cannot print the lessons and you cannot download (or cache) the lessons onto your hard drive.

2) Purchase the appropriate amount of copies of this book for your students.

Please understand that we can only afford to continue to maintain our websites and create new and innovation learning materials if we can be reimbursed for our time and expense. The only ways we can be reimbursed are through the ads on our sites and the purchase of our books. Your assistance in this area is greatly appreciated!

How can you help support Coolmath? Please ask your school and your district to create links on their official websites to Coolmath.com (or any of our other sites). These links help our rankings with search engines such as Google. Higher rankings help new people find us… And helping as many people as possible is our goal!

For more information about copyrights and fair use, a good resource is from the Standford University Library:

http://fairuse.stanford.edu/Copyright_and_Fair_Use_Overview/index.html

Thanks for your interest in Coolmath… And thanks again for reading this. We really appreciate teachers like you!

Coolmath Algebra – Part 1
Table of Contents

YOUR MATH SURVIVAL GUIDE

::: 1   I Was a Mathphobe! 3
::: 2   Do You Hate Math? Or are You Just Afraid of It? 7
::: 3   Think You Stink at Math? 9
::: 4   Do You Want to be Successful? 13
::: 5   Change Your Attitude! 17
::: 6   How to be a Successful Student 19
::: 7   How to Study for a Math Test 21
::: 8   Dealing With Anxiety 23
::: 9   How to Use This Book 29
::: 10   Frequently Asked Questions 31

EXPONENTS AND RADICALS

::: 1   Exponents – Remember These? 35
::: 2   Exponent Rules – Rule #1 38
::: 3   Exponent Rules – Rule #2 41
::: 4   Exponent Rules – Rule #3 46
::: 5   Exponent Rules – Rule #4 48
::: 6   Exponent Rules – Putting Rules #1-4 Together 51
::: 7   Exponent Rules – Review 54
::: 8   Exponent Rules – Rule #5 58
::: 9   Exponent Rules – Rule #6 61
::: 10   Radicals – A Review of Radicals 64
::: 11   Radicals – Rules for Radicals 70
::: 12   Radicals – Rewriting Radicals 73
::: 13   Radicals – Adding & Subtracting Radicals 78
::: 14   Radicals – Multiplying Messier Radicals 80
::: 15   Radicals – Rationalizing Denominators 81
::: 16   Radicals – Fractional Exponents 85

POLYNOMIALS, FACTORING AND DIVISION

::: 1   Polynomials – Sticking Numbers In 95
::: 2   Polynomials – What's a Polynomial, Anyway? 96
::: 3   Polynomials – Some Math Words to Know 97
::: 4   Polynomials – Adding & Subtracting 101
::: 5   Polynomials – Multiplying Easy Ones 106
::: 6   Polynomials – Multiplying with FOIL 108
::: 7   Polynomials – Multiplying Messier Ones 111
::: 8   Factoring – What's a Factor Again? 113
::: 9   Factoring – Undoing the Distributive Property 114
::: 10   Factoring – Intro to Trinomials 118
::: 11   Factoring – Trinomials – Undoing FOIL 121
::: 12   Factoring – Harder Trinomials 123
::: 13   Factoring – Special Guys 144
::: 14   Factoring – By Grouping 149
::: 15   Factoring – A Final Overview 153
::: 16   Division – Dividing by Monomials 157
::: 17   Division – Long Division 160
::: 18   Division – Freaky Things That Can Happen (Part 1) . . 167
::: 19   Division – Freaky Things That Can Happen (Part 2) . . 170

SOLVING EQUATIONS AND INEQUALITIES

::: 1   Solving Equations – Keep It Balanced 178
::: 2   Solving Equations – What To Do - Part 1 180
::: 3   Solving Equations – What To Do - Part 2 182
::: 4   Solving Equations – What To Do - Part 3 –
      Putting Parts 1 and 2 Together 188
::: 5   Solving Equations – What To Do – Messier Ones . . . 191
::: 6   Solving Equations – Dealing With Fractions &
      Decimals 194
::: 7   Solving Inequalities – What Your Answers Will Look
      Like (Intervals) 201
::: 8   Solving Inequalities – Set-Builder Notation 205
::: 9   Solving Inequalities – Interval Notation 207
::: 10   Solving Inequalities – Solving Basic Guys 211
::: 11   Solving Inequalities – The Freaky Thing 215
::: 11   Solving Inequalities – Compound Inequalities 219

LINES

- ::: 1   The Cartesian Coordinate System 228
- ::: 2   Plotting Points 229
- ::: 3   Graphing Lines Using Intercepts 232
- ::: 4   What's the Slope of a Line? 237
- ::: 5   Finding the Slope of a Line from the Graph 239
- ::: 6   Finding the Slope of a Line from Two Points 242
- ::: 7   Equations of Lines (Graphing Method 2) 245
- ::: 8   Horizontal & Vertical Lines 248
- ::: 9   Graphing Overview 251
- ::: 10   Finding the Slope from the Equation of a Line 256
- ::: 11   Finding the Equation of a Line
  Given a Point and a Slope 259
- ::: 12   Finding the Equation of a Line Given Two Points 262
- ::: 13   Parallel Lines 265
- ::: 14   Perpendicular Lines 268
- ::: 15   Graphing Line Inequalities 272

THE BACK OF THE BOOK

- ::: 1   The Answers 284

YOUR MATH SURVIVAL GUIDE

I Was a Mathphobe!

Hey, I used to hate math and I even thought I was terrible at it! And now I'm one of the most famous math geeks on the planet... *There's* something to brag about, Baby!

Here's my story:

My only memory of math in elementary school is listening to a tape of a man saying, "Three times four is.... Four times four is... Five times four is... Blah blah blah." It was one of those drills where you had to write down the answers before he asked the next one. It just occurred to me... Why couldn't my teacher have asked us these questions? Why on earth did they need a tape for this?! Anyway, that's all I remember.

But, seventh grade – boy, do I remember seventh grade! Much to my chagrin, they stuck me in one of those "gifted" programs. You know the ones – where you have to do twice as much work as the other kids and get lower grades as a reward. This never did make sense to me. So, I was in something called 7X Math. I guess the "X" was put in there as some sort of sick algebra joke. It was a cruel irony to say the least. I remember this class very well and I remember being completely clueless the entire time. I also remember how it felt to have "F" exams passed back to me and seeing that everyone around me seemed to be getting A's and B's. How could these students understand all the hieroglyphics and cave drawings the teacher kept scribbling all over the board? I remember the teacher too... Oh... I remember him. Mr. Ubbernerd (not his real name). Unfortunately, our class was right after lunch. He always managed to have at least half a pound of white Weber's bread left in his front teeth. And there was this little blob of spit... As he talked, it would string from the middle of his upper lip to his lower... up... down... up... down. It was mesmerizing. Perhaps this is why I failed the class – spit blob obsession.

My next math teacher (I think it was the second half of seventh grade) was nice. I don't remember learning any math, particularly, but I do remember that it wasn't safe to sit in the front because he sprayed spit when he talked. (Do you see a "too much saliva" theme going on here too? What's with that?)

Now, on to eight grade – Prealgebra. I had math during 7th period and there was a kid named David in our class. I'm sure you had a kid like David in your grade. He was the kid that always orchestrated the dropping of books at exactly 2:15, the kid who knew how to convert a Bic pen into a pellet shooter and the kid who always had enough spit for 18 spit wads (all to be aimed at the classroom clock). That kid. My teacher hated that kid and the rest of the class along with him. So, between David and what seemed to be a chronic case of PMS on my teacher's part, I didn't learn any math that year.

Ninth grade – Prealgebra yet again. Does this mean that I failed 8th grade math? I think it does even though no one really said that at the time. This year went pretty well. I had a good teacher and I remember that I got some good grades. Things were looking up for me – mathematically speaking.

Then came tenth grade – Algebra 1. The teacher told us that we could either pay attention or sleep, just as long as we didn't talk. So, I slept. Hey, it was right before lunch and my blood sugar was dropping. I didn't do any homework yet I still, somehow, miraculously managed to squeak out C-'s on my tests – just barely enough. That was fine with me after what I'd been through. I just wanted to get the heck out of there!

I spent the next several years successfully avoiding math at all costs. At one point, I thought about majoring in Chemistry. I had a fantastic chemistry teacher and you could mix wildly colored things and make them smoke. Fun stuff. So, I sent away for information from my two local state colleges… Ouch! They both said that I'd have to take two years of Calculus. TWO YEARS OF CALCULUS!! I figured that I'd never be able to get through that and dropped the idea. (By the way, I now TEACH Calculus.)

Then it happened. In the fall of 1985, I was forced (at gunpoint – I swear) by my college to take a math class. It was Intermediate Algebra. I had to eat three Rolaids just so I could look at the schedule to pick a class time. Over the years, I had grown to view math in the same way as things like cooties and the Ebola virus – avoidance at all cost! But, I wanted to go to college… and I hadn't taken enough math in high school (cootie avoidance)… So, I was stuck.

After two packs of Rolaids and some Imodium-AD, I finally picked the class – late morning, so I could sleep in, of course. Hey, I was a serious student!

I still remember that first class… I didn't know whether I was going to throw-up, pass out or start crying. The teacher kept saying, "… and you remember THIS from last semester…" Last semester… Last semester? I didn't take any math last semester! Oh my GOSH! I was supposed to take MATH last semester?!

I leaned over and whispered to the student next to me, "Last semester? Do you know what he's doing?" She quickly shook her head, "No." She had the same horrified look on her face as I did.

The teacher was in rare form that day, my friend – all hopped up on coffee and donuts and covered from head to toe with chalk dust… "And you remember this type of linear blah-blah whose graph is clearly blah blah blah…" "Clearly." Uh… Yeah. Good thing I had the Rolaids with me. This guy was a major grouch who obviously had some sort of deficient childhood. Yes, he had scared the living crud out of me.

After class, the other clueless student and I cautiously approached the teacher – much like one would approach a live grenade or a baby that was accidentally fed chili. We got up our nerve and told him that neither of us had taken any math the previous semester and that we didn't recognize anything he had just done on the chalkboard. He gruffly told us that we'd never be able to pass his class and that we should drop and take an easier one. He wasn't exactly kind about it. I think his exact response was, "You're going to fail this class. Get out!"

Boy, were we mad! We got out in the hallway and agreed that he wasn't going to chase US off! We were going to show HIM! The nerve of that guy! Luckily, we decided to NOT try to run him over in the parking lot. Hey, things like that have consequences!

We studied and studied… And we both got A's on the first test! To this day, I'll never forget having that "93" paper handed back to me. I can still picture it. Boy, what a great feeling that was.

So, after a LOT of hard work, I ended up getting a B in that class. (I would have gotten an A, but after ripping a 93% on the first test, I got cocky and didn't study for the second one… I ate a big D- that day and learned a big lesson!)

But, do you really know what I learned that semester? Math wasn't so bad after all. In fact, it was pretty fun! I guess I had really never given it a chance. Heck, who would have guessed that I could be really good at it?

By the way, that grumpy professor turned out to be a really nice guy who gave me a lot of extra help. He even talked me into becoming a college math teacher. And that other initially clueless student turned out to be the best study-buddy anyone could ask for. She got an A that semester and is now a high school math teacher.

It just goes to show you… You never know where you'll end up. ANYTHING can happen. You might even end up LIKING math! But, don't worry… I'm not going to try to turn you into a math major! Let's just get you through this so you can go on to live a happy life.

Do You Hate Math?
Or Are You Just Afraid of It?

Hate or afraid – it's kind of the same thing.

I hate spiders… Why? Because I'm afraid of them. It doesn't matter that without spiders the world would be covered with bugs. I don't care about that. I hate them anyway. They're creepy and have thick, hairy legs. When I see one, it's him or me – I go into attack mode. The way I see it, if he's really big and I don't kill him, I'll have to move out of my house… Because I'll know he's in there… somewhere… waiting to kill me in my sleep… taunting me… and making baby spiders.

Last year, I actually saw a spider who only had three legs – one on the left (his left, not mine) and two on the right. I let him live. Hey, any spider who had survived a tragedy that ripped 5 legs off (or worse – five individual traumas each taking one leg), had really earned the right to live. That spider was a miracle! So, I let him get away – albeit, very slowly.

What was I talking about? Oh, yeah… math! Hate or fear: the result is the same – when you see a math book, you scream and jump onto the nearest chair. Wait… That's me with spiders. How about this? You get sick to your stomach and develop a nervous twitch in your left eye while little beads of sweat sprout on your upper lip.

I know. I was there. I hated math. I thought I was terrible at it too. So, I know how you feel. I know how it feels to stare at a chalkboard full of math that may as well be in a foreign language. I know how it feels to sit and stare at a page full of math problems and not even be able to do the first one. I know how it feels to be so overwhelmed and frustrated that tears start flowing. I know.

But, it may not be that you hate math… and it may not be that you are afraid of math… It may just be that you think you stink at math! Keep reading…

Think You Stink at Math?

Do you think you're bad in math? If you're reading this page, I'll bet you do. It's also a good bet that it someone **told** you that you're bad at math.

Most people can think of one thing, one incident, one terrible haunting memory that has made them think they stink at this stuff. If this is you, take a minute and write down what happened and how it made you feel. Here's an empty spot. (I'll wait.)

So, you think you're bad in math? Well, guess what? You're wrong! DEAD WRONG! And, if someone told you that you are bad in math, *they* were wrong! DEAD WRONG!

You're NOT bad in math -- You just haven't done well in math in the past. It's doesn't mean you can't do it. It doesn't mean that you aren't good at it!

Grab a piece of paper and write this down... Go on! I'll wait:

It's not that I'm bad in math, it's just that I've had bad experiences with math!

Now, put that piece of paper in the front of your math notebook and look at it everyday before math class until you really believe it!

You are in good company with people who've been told that they stink at stuff.

Check out this list:

- **Albert Einstein** was four years old before he could speak and seven before he could read.

- As a boy **Thomas Edison** was told by his teachers that he was too stupid to learn anything.

- **Werner von Braun**, one of our most important rocket scientists from 1930 to 1970, flunked ninth-grade algebra. (Do you KNOW how much algebra you need to know to do rocket science? Dang!)

- **Winston Churchill** failed the sixth grade.

- **Leo Tolstoy**, author of War and Peace, flunked out of college.

- **Louis Pasteur** was rated mediocre in chemistry when he attended the Royal College. He went on to discover that "germs" cause disease prompting hospitals to start sanitizing things. He also invented milk pasteurization and cured rabies. (Yeah, he was mediocre, alright. Clearly, pretty lazy too. He only changed the world.)

- **Walt Disney** was fired by a newspaper editor because he had "no good ideas." (Yeah, Disneyland and animated cartoons were really bad ideas.)

- **Gwendolyn Sykes**, the Chief Financial Officer of NASA, failed Algebra! Now, she's in charge of the finances for one of the biggest companies around.

- **Paul Orfalea**, founder of Kinkos, was labeled as "retarded" in elementary school. He isn't, of course. He is dyslexic though, but he doesn't let that stop him.

- **Robert Kiyosaki**, author of the all-time best selling personal finance book, *Rich Dad, Poor Dad*, failed English twice in high school.

I wouldn't exactly put myself on the same list as the people above, but I failed Algebra too and now I'm a semi-famous math geek and make my living teaching the stuff.

So, put all the negative crud that someone else attached to you far behind you… It's time to move on to SUCCESS! **You CAN do it and you WILL do it.** It's just going to take some hard work and a positive attitude.

Do You Want to be Successful?

Of course you do! And I'm not talking about just being successful in your math classes. I'm talking about being a successful person IN EVERYTHING! So, do you want to be successful?

You may think that this was a silly question. No one daydreams about being unsuccessful. Let's see… I'm hoping to barely get by, live pay check to pay check and have a job I don't like and be, generally, unhappy. No way! No one really thinks that… But, it happens to people anyway… All the time.

This may be the most important thing I say in the whole book…

Having success is a decision we can make for ourselves.

Let's take a minute… I want you to write down your dream. What are you dreaming of? What are you striving for? Is it your dream job? Is it your dream house? What do you want for your future? And I want you to aim high! If you aim for the sky and only make it 80% of the way, it will still be a lot higher than if you started by aiming for mediocrity.

I'll wait while you write down your dream… Here's a blank spot to do it in…

My dream:

Read it 5 times – read it out loud. Then, close your eyes for 5 minutes and think about it. Visualize it!

Now, I'm going to tell you how you can get it. (By the way, if you're thinking, "Hey, this isn't talking about algebra." Yes, it is! Just wait.)

Highly successful people have 6 things:

- **Creativity**
- **The ability to think and figure things out**
- **The ability to self-teach**
- **Confidence**
- **A positive attitude**
- **DRIVE!**

Let's look at each one.

1) Creativity

When most people think of creativity, they think of artists, dancers and writers… But, the most successful people in business, engineering, science and medicine are highly creative! When Donald Trump is putting together a deal, he's got to be able to think out of the box. He even wrote the bestselling business book of all time called "The Art of the Deal." And what does it take to create something new in science? That's right… Creativity!

2) The ability to think and figure things out

Thinking and figuring things out isn't just for science and business. Working out a dance routine requires planning and thinking. Writing takes a LOT of thinking. In fact, everything that you would consider an "art" takes thinking and planning.

Whether it's a science, an art, business or something else, having both creativity and the ability to think and figure things out makes for a killer combination. But, this isn't all that's needed to be successful... You still need more!

3) The ability to self-teach

When you're close to the top or at the top, there's no longer anyone around to teach you what you need to know next. Those who make it to the top and stay there are the ones who figure out what they need to learn next and learn it on their own. This is especially true for someone setting out to create something that's never been done before!

Also, it will be very important, no matter what your first "real" job ends up being, that you be able to learn things quickly and, yes, even on your own. Suppose two people are hired at the same time for the same type of job. Both are supplied with the same introductory information to perform his/her job. Person #1 keeps bothering the boss asking question after question. Person #2 carefully reviews the materials provided and starts working - perhaps just asking a couple of thoughtful and intelligent questions. If you were the boss, which new employee would impress you the most?

Of course, asking questions is often very necessary, but you'll want to try to find the answer on your own before asking. The last thing you want your boss to say is, "That's on page 2 of your instruction package." Then you look like a royal doofus – something to be avoided at a new job. Don't say I never gave you any good advice. Avoid looking like a royal doofus.

4) Confidence

You may have it or you may not. You may have it in some areas and not in others. It sure seems like some people were just born confident. You see them walking around school acting like they've got it all together. In reality, they're probably just better at ACTING confident and, on the inside, they may feel differently. The great thing is that confidence can be built from items 1, 2 and 3 above!

5) A positive attitude

Have you ever heard the phrase "Bloom where you are planted?" No? OK, pretend that you're a little flower seed getting blown down an old paved road... You fall in a crack. Well, dang it, BLOOM ANYWAY! Of course, it would have been nice to have been planted in a nice pot with nutritious soil just the right amount of water... But, you got stuck with a crack in the road, so make the most of it!

I'm sure that a math class is not where you'd like to be spending your time. But, you don't have much of a choice in the matter, do you? You may really like the idea of being in school and learning... But not THIS stuff!

There comes a time in life when you have to decide what kind of person you are going to be. Are you the type that will gripe and complain the whole time? Or are you the type that will make the best of the situation and find a way to use it to your benefit?

Successful people are always the ones to look at a seemingly unpleasant situation or a bad turn of events and say, "How am I going to use this to my advantage?" They will always find a way to make the most out of everything.

When life gives you lemons, make lemonade – AND SELL IT!

6) Drive

Highly successful people set their goals... and they aim high. They know what they want and they go after it. They want it badly and are willing to work very hard to get it!

Six things... That's it.

Now, let's focus on your attitude...

Change Your Attitude!

So, you're stuck taking a class and having to learn stuff that you, most likely, will never need. Why do you have to even take this class?! I mean, it's all SO unfair! This crud is standing between you and your dreams!

Well, everyone on the planet has decided that you need a certain amount of math to get out of high school and that you need a certain amount of math to get a college degree. That's the deal. Why do you think this is? Is it because you'll need math for your job? Not likely. So what is it?

Math trains you to think... and to figure things out.

OK, so you say you've heard THAT line before... and you're not buying it.

You want to be a successful person, right? A successful person would figure out a way to use a class like this to his or her advantage. A successful person would want to take this seemingly bad situation and twist it around. A successful person would take these lemons, make lemonade AND SELL IT! And YOU are going to be a successful person!

So, here's the silver bullet – the secret to success – the key to surviving this algebra thing:

It's not about the math!

You're not in a math class!

THIS IS A CLASS IN SUCCESS TRAINING!

You're going to use your algebra class to learn how to be successful. You're going to learn how to be creative, how to think and figure things out and how to self-teach (this is the most important one). It just so happens that the subject you're going to use to learn these things is Algebra.

The confidence will come quickly as you conquer this algebra stuff. Hey, if you can learn this, you can learn ANYTHING. You'll attack the rest of your classes and rip A's. Nothing will scare you anymore (except, maybe, spiders).

The positive attitude and the drive are up to you. These are things that have to come from deep inside YOU! These are your decisions… All you have to do is to decide to have them and they are yours… and no one can take them away! These are the two most important things to get you started.

I know you're still skeptical at this point, but bear with me… and trust me. I've taken thousands of mathphobes worse than you and turned them into savage algebra animals who can rip through the most treacherous of algebra exams with relative ease!

How to be a Successful Student

1) Always attend the first class meeting! This lets you know what the teacher is like and what is expected of you.

2) Read the class syllabus! (Or whatever the teacher passes out the first week) This will let you know all the rules regarding absences, exams, etc.

3) Be on time for class! In fact, always try to be a little early, so you can get out all your stuff.

4) Don't miss class unless you are really sick (nobody wants your germs!). Your teacher can explain something to you in a fraction of the time that it would take you to figure it out on your own (or even with the help of a tutor.)

5) If you do have to miss a class, always call a classmate (before you return to class!) to find out what you missed and if your teacher assigned anything that will be due when you return.

6) During class, always have your calculator on your desk and have your text book out. Teachers often do problems out of the book as examples.

7) If the teacher is making some sort of computation, work along with him/her.

8) Take very neat class notes. Write down everything the teacher writes down and try to write down most of what he/she says. Put stars by problems or points that your teacher stresses or get excited about. These are good potential exam questions!

9) Participate and ask questions!

10) Do your homework the same day that you hear the lecture on the material! If that isn't possible, always be sure to do the homework before you go to the next class.

11) Make friends in the class and study with them! I.E. Form well-balanced study groups. A good study group consists of 4 or 5 students with a range of capabilities. (Students getting D's and F's should never study together - This doesn't benefit anybody. It just turns out to be a big pity party.)

12) The second that you start to feel overwhelmed with the material (ex: you didn't understand a thing the teacher said or you can't do the assignment that night) get help! Go to your math learning center, get a tutor, ask for help from a classmate and go to your teacher's office!!

13) Get in the proper frame of mind! <u>This class is your job.</u> How much effort are you putting forth? Do you always clock in late or do you just not show up? If this class was **really** your job, would you get fired or would you be up for a raise?

How to Study for a Math Test

When studying for an algebra test, you have two main goals:

- Learn the material so you can do well on the exam.

- Learn the material well enough so you will still know it next semester!!! (Most of you will be taking more math. These classes ALWAYS depend on the material you learned the previous semester! If you don't really learn it (i.e. not just cramming for the exam), you'll crash and burn in your next class!

Tip #1:
Have all memorizing done *a couple of days before the exam...* BUT, *you should UNDERSTAND what's going on! Trying to just memorize it never lasts.*

Tip #2:
USE FLASH CARDS FOR MEMORIZATION OF FORMULAS AND RULES!!!

---

1) Starting out:

- Look over lecture notes.
    - REWORK EXAMPLES!!
- Look over homework.

2) Make an exam for yourself (or better yet, for a study partner):

- Take it after a delay period - So you won't remember where you got the problems - If you take the exam too soon, you may think you know the material better then you do! (*This should be done at least TWO (2) days before the exam - NOT the night before or you'll freak yourself out!*)

> **NOTE:** It is extremely important that you be able to do the problems *without* knowing what section they came out of!! Be sure to mix the problems up when you are practicing!

3) Restudy:

- Go back over what you had trouble with on your practice exam. This is the stuff that you didn't absorb well enough from just doing your homework.

4) The afternoon before exam day:

- *Read through your lecture notes and think!* Work some problems and review memorizing.

5) The night before exam day:

- Do something fun ----------- But not *too* much fun! 8-)

6) One hour before exam:

- Glance over flash cards and don't talk to classmates -- They may say something to confuse you or make you nervous. 8-)

> # Above all → DON'T CRAM!!!

Anything you try to learn at the last minute (that means the night before) will dribble out your left ear when you get nervous!

Dealing with Anxiety

Most students experience anxiety over math tests. It's normal. In fact, studies show that you should be a bit anxious before and during exams because it makes you perform better. So, a little anxiety is a good thing. What isn't good is when the anxiety gets so bad that it gives you a sick stomach and makes you cry! This level of anxiety can interfere with your performance. As you'll read later, I don't think a case of nerves can drop an A student down to an F, but I do think it can drop you to a B or C based on nervous mistakes like 2 x 3 = 5 or dropping a negative sign.

The only students who don't have even a little test anxiety are the ones who know they're going to fail and don't care.

Heck, I've even had test anxiety! I'm sure you can only imagine how many math tests I've had to take in my lifetime. I've been through the gambit of anxieties… the sleepless night, the upset stomach, the headache, the stiff neck, the tears… It wasn't pretty stuff.

But, I learned a very important lesson one day. I had three upper division (college) math classes one semester (actually, most semesters), so I had three math finals in one week to look forward to. Of course, I had studied well for all of them, but by the end of the second one, I was fried! My brain was cooked. I was so completely over the whole thing. While I was leaving campus after final exam #2, I ran into the professor who was giving final exam #3 the next day. He smiled and asked me if I was ready for his final. I looked at him and said, "Right now, I'm so tired that I don't even care."

I went home, studied a bit more and slept. The next morning I was still fried – sleep hadn't helped. I dragged myself over to school for the last final exam… and, really, I was too tired to care how I did! That was a first for me. I'd always been really competitive with myself about my math grades. (Can you say "geek"?) That day, I was too tired to care… and it was the very first math test I'd taken where I wasn't the least bit nervous! It was great. I just calmly sat there and easily worked the problems -- a snap. In fact, I got a perfect paper… and one of those problems was a killer! But, I figured it out.

After that, tests weren't that bad… I realized that I didn't have to get myself all worked up over them.

But, then came my thesis defense! For my master's degree in math, I had to write a thesis. This was, basically, a 117 page book that contained a 63 page proof. (Geek!) The other 54 pages contained my explanations of the math used in the proof. It took me about 8 months to write it and it had to be accepted or I wasn't going to get my degree. So, this was a BIG deal. For the thesis "defense" I had to present and explain the proof to a group of 17 people: 12 professors (with PhD's) and 5 other graduate students... After, they got to ask questions and I had to know the answers. The whole thing was to take about an hour. Man, was I nervous!! In fact, I had been nervous about the defense for the last EIGHT MONTHS!

I'll never forget something that happened while I was driving over to school that morning... It suddenly occurred to me... I was going to have to do the defense no matter what... And I could do it while being nervous... Or I could do it while being calm. Either way, it was going to happen! I realized that I had a choice: be nervous or be calm... Calm would be so much more pleasant. So, I instantly calmed down and stayed that way the entire time. It was amazing. Just a simple decision and it worked!

You can make the same decision when you're taking math tests! I know that this may not seem like an easy thing for you though, so here are some exercises you can do that will help. Just like anything else, learning to be calm will take practice. The more you do these, the better you'll get! The most important thing for you to realize is that there IS something you can do to reduce your math anxiety.

Before tests (especially the night before) and while studying:

Visualization

Effectively using visualization is a two-parter: the first way is for relaxation and the second is in preparing for the future.

Let's first talk about visualization for relaxation. This can be a quickie thing that you do in your classroom right before a test, or the night before the test, or while you're waiting in line somewhere, or while you're sitting in a traffic jam... Or it can be done much like meditation where you are sitting or lying in a quiet place.

Close your eyes (unless, of course, you are driving -- or trying to read this) and picture yourself in a beautiful nature setting like the beach, the mountains or a meadow full of flowers. My favorite place is the beach and it's my book, so let's go there!

Visualize, smell, hear and feel every part of it. You're sitting on the warm sand with your shoes off... You can feel the warm sand between your toes... You are looking out at the waves as they break on the shore... Hear that soft, crashing sound of the surf and the seagulls... Feel the cool breeze hitting your face... Pick up a handful of warm sand and feel it slowly sift out between your fingers... Smell the clean, salty ocean air... This is a safe place... No cares... No worries... Just you and the beach... Peaceful... Relaxing... Feel the stress drain out of you as you soak up the warmth of the sand and the smell of the cool air...

Now that you've read it, try it yourself. Read it back through one more time... Then, close your eyes and try it...

Now, let's talk about visualization for success. This will best be done during quick study breaks, the night before a test and while you're driving and/or walking to class to take the test. Definitely combine it with your visualization for relaxation – either before or after, whatever is best for you.

Close your eyes... Picture yourself taking the math test... Sitting in your seat in the classroom... You're very calm and working the problems without anxiety... Your mind is clear and working at its best... You are remembering everything you studied... Picture yourself successfully working the types of problems you'll be getting... After you've completed the exam, picture a big red "A" and "Great job!" written at the top of the first page.

Relaxation Exercises

Sometimes it takes a lot of practice to learn how to relax, especially if you are a stressed out student. You probably don't even realize that the muscles in your back, neck and shoulders are all knotted up. The following are all exercises that will help you relax -- some are more time-consuming and some are quick things you can do while driving or before an exam. Work these into your daily routine and practice, practice, practice.

Head to Toe Inventory
This exercise is a great thing to do when you have 20 minutes or so, like before bedtime or when you are taking a study break. Lay on a bed or somewhere else that's really comfortable or sit up straight in a comfy chair. Put on some nice soothing music (something without vocals is best) or one of those "nature sounds" CDs or just have it quiet. If "quiet" in your house is impossible, get some earplugs.

What you're going to be doing is working your way through all the major muscle groups in your body -- first tightening them, then, letting them completely relax.

Here's the order...

Your face... your neck... your shoulders... your arms... back to your shoulders and upper back... your torso (chest, abs, lower back)... your caboose... your legs... your feet.

Then, once you're all mushy and relaxed, just lay still and enjoy.

Get Heavy
This is another one that's good when you have 20 minutes or so to really relax. Lie down or sit somewhere comfortable (sit up straight). Again, make things quiet or put on some mellow "new age" music or "nature sounds."

Working from your feet up, you are going to concentrate on making parts of your body really heavy... and, when we are on an area, I want you to imagine all the blood in your body rushing to that area.

First, your legs... Imagine all the blood in your body rushing to your legs and feel them get heavier and heavier. Don't push on them or move them at all. You can't move them, they are too heavy. When you feel the heaviness and the warmth of the blood rushing through them, move on... Next comes your core (your torso)... Then, your arms... When your body is heavy, imagine your head feeling cool and refreshed. Imagine a cool breeze blowing across your forehead and through your hair. Just lay and enjoy.

Take a 4 Count
This one is really simple and can be done anywhere even for just a minute or so and even DURING an exam... If you can't do a problem and start to freak out, this is a great one! Close your eyes (unless you're driving, silly!)... Slowly breathe in and count 1... 2... 3... 4... Now, slowly exhale and count 4... 3... 2... 1... Do this at a pace that you're comfortable with -- you don't want to hyperventilate! Don't let your mind wander. Concentrate on those numbers.

Good In, Bad Out
This one is very similar to "Take a 4 Count," but this one uses a bit of imagination. Again, you can do this one anywhere and for even just a brief time like during a test. Close your eyes (if you can)... Slowly breathe in and imagine that you are breathing in nothing but good stuff - positive thoughts, good things, pure air, relaxation... Now, slowly exhale and imagine that you are blowing out all your stress, bad thoughts, negativity, bad air. Again, don't hyperventilate! Don't let your mind wander. Concentrate on good in and bad out.

Or, you can just scream "serenity now" right in the middle of your math test! (Just kidding. That doesn't work and your math teacher probably won't appreciate it.)

Now, I have to say something tough here… and this is after seeing and talking to thousands of students over the years… Anxiety cannot take a student who really knows the material and make him/her completely fail a test. I've talked to MANY students who, upon receiving an F on a test, tell me that they "really knew the material" but just got nervous and blanked out. After doing a little digging, it always turns out that they really didn't know the material as well as they thought they did. The problem mostly occurs because students will look over their notes and see that it all looks very familiar… So, they make the assumption that they know the stuff. But, looking at completed problems is very different than looking at a bunch of questions that aren't in the same order as the sections in the book and be able to work them cold.

A case of nerves cannot drop an A or B student (one who really knows the stuff) down to an F. But, it can drop you a grade or two via a bunch of little arithmetic mistakes and things like dropping negative signs.

BUT… know this:
If you are taking a math test and you HAVEN'T studied as much as you should have, you SHOULD be nervous… In fact, if you haven't studied enough, I WANT you to be nervous and sick to your stomach! That's right. I want tears to start pouring. I want that test to be such a miserable experience for you that you will study your caboose off for the next one so you can do your best! I want the best for you and I want YOU to want the best for you too. You can't conquer math unless you try and try HARD! Make… it… happen!

Dealing with Anxiety

How to Use This Book

READ THE WORDS!

That means, don't just look and the stuff with numbers and x's. **Read the words too!** Hey, I say some pretty important stuff with those words.

I know students. You're busy and you're impatient to just get this stuff. I've had thousands of my own students use this book... and I've had the opportunity to watch them read it during class. I learned pretty quickly that most students don't take the time to read the words. Oh, I'd get called over to answer a question... and the answer was in the paragraph on the page they just (supposedly) read. Busted!

But, don't worry. There really aren't that many words and none of them are that big (haha). It's not like a regular math book where you have huge paragraphs in 8 point font with dozens of long math words. It's just me... It'll be just like I'm talking to you in person. It'll be easy.

Read the words too and you'll get everything twice as fast. TRUST ME!

WRITE IN IT!

During each section, there will be spaces right on the page for you to try some problems for yourself... Write in the book! Don't do the work on a separate page. Do it in the book.

Why? OK, this is going to sound silly... The reason is because it psychologically merges you with the book and, thus, with the math. Yeah, I don't say goofy-psycho-babble stuff very often, but it's really true in this case. You will feel more connected with the book and with me if you work along and write in the spaces provided.

BACK UP!

Let's say that you're having troubles with finding the equation of a line that is perpendicular to another given line. (Sorry, I didn't mean to give you a headache so soon! Bear with me.) This kind of problem might not be your issue… It may be that you aren't comfortable with how to find the slope of a line (which is the first step). If you don't go back to learn that part properly, you've got no hope of doing the harder problem. So, be willing to back up a few sections (when you need to) and do some review. It will take a little more time at first, but it will pay off in the long run.

GO SLOWLY!

There are no prizes for who can read the math book the fastest. Take your time. As you read, really go slowly and always be thinking about what you are reading.

Follow along with my examples – don't just skim them. Take the time to follow each one of my steps.

It takes time to learn to do something really well. No one learns to play the piano overnight. It takes time and practice. **Be patient. You'll get it!!**

Frequently Asked Questions

Why isn't this book typed? What's the matter, were you too cheap or too lazy to get it typed?

I get this question all the time, although not put quite so brutally... But, I know what they are thinking.

The answer is very simple! I remember what it was like to open up a math textbook and see all those graphs and all that little typed font... It always made me think, "This math was done by a machine and not by a person. I won't be able to do it." To me, math books always looked inhuman and impossible!

This book wasn't done by a machine... and it wasn't written by some math geek robot... It was written by me. It's just me explaining the stuff to you as if I was sitting right there next to you at your desk. It's human.

The answer to the follow-up question is "Yes, my hand hurt for a long time."

What's Coolmath?

Coolmath.com is a website that I started in the spring of 1997. Since then, I've added a ton of content and a bunch of other sites and we're currently helping about **100,000 students a DAY**!

I now have several other sites:

Coolmath4kids.com
Coolmath-Games.com
SpikesGameZone.com
ScienceMonster.com
FinanceFREAK.com
TotallyStressedOut.com

And I'm working on StudentSuccessWEB.com... But, it isn't up yet.

What are Karen's official qualifications?

Eh, this is the boring stuff. But, if you're interested... I have a BA and MS in Mathematics from California State University, Long Beach. I tutored many Algebra students while I was a student.

I stayed on as a teacher at CSULB and taught Algebra and Math for Elementary Teachers. Then, I got a full-time job at a local community college where I've taught just about everything from Algebra to Calculus. In total, I have 14 years of teaching experience. During the last five years, I've read a lot of books on the psychology of learning and even several business books on how to motivate people. Teaching is a lot more than just the math.

EXPONENTS
-AND-
RADICALS

Exponents - Remember these?

Remember from your arithmetic days (or is that daze?) what this means?

$$2^3$$

That's three 2's all multiplied together:

$$2^3 = 2 \cdot 2 \cdot 2 = 8$$

As you know by now, in Algebra, we work with that unknown guy... Mr. X!

The thing to remember is that x is a number -- we just don't know which one.

So, all the stuff you learned in arithmetic works here too!

$$x^3 = x \cdot x \cdot x$$

What if we stick a 5 in front of this thing?

$$5x^3$$

The 5 is called a coefficient (because it's a number in front of an x guy) and it's just multiplied in with the x's.)

$$5x^3 = 5 \cdot x \cdot x \cdot x$$

Remember that x is some mystery number... What would we get if we let $x = 3$?

$$5x^3 = 5(3)^3 = 5 \cdot 3 \cdot 3 \cdot 3 = 135$$

What if $x = -2$? Be careful!

$$5x^3 = 5(-2)^3 = 5(-2)(-2)(-2) = -40$$

Try it:

Write out what $3x^4$ means:

$3xxxx$

Let $x = 2$ and simplify:

$3(2)(2)(2)(2) = 48$

Let $x = -5$ and simplify:

$3(-5)(-5)(-5)(-5) = 1875$

Here's something a little messier:

What does this thing mean?

$$100n^2 m^6$$

The number hangs around in front... and we can expand out those exponents:

$$100 \cdot n \cdot n \cdot m \cdot m \cdot m \cdot m \cdot m \cdot m$$

So, why do we have exponents?

Look at this thing!

$$x^{590}$$

Glad I don't have to write that thing out!
How about working the other way around?
Let's simplify this:

$$7xxxxww$$

The 7 hangs around in front... and we just count up the letters:

$$7x^4w^2$$

Your turn:

Simplify $8aaabccccc$

$8A^3bc^5$

FOR MORE ALGEBRA PRACTICE PROBLEMS, CHECK OUT MY

Algebra Crunchers

Generate an endless number of algebra problems -- with hints and answers, so you can check your work!

Coolmath.com/crunchers

Exponents - Remember These?

Exponent Rules - Rule #1

Can we add these guys?
$$x^2 + x^3$$

No way, dude! Not like terms!

So... can we multiply them?
$$x^2 \cdot x^3$$

Totally! Just write out what each one means and see what happens!

$$x^2 \cdot x^3 = \underbrace{x \cdot x \cdot x \cdot x \cdot x}_{\text{5 of them}} = x^5$$

That wasn't bad.
What about this guy?
$$w^3 \cdot w^4$$

$$w^3 \cdot w^4 = w \cdot w \cdot w \cdot w \cdot w \cdot w \cdot w = w^7$$

Try it:

base → $y \cdot y^6 \qquad y^7$

this 4 stands for one

Glad I don't have to write that thing out!
How about working the other way around?
Let's simplify this:

$$7xxxxww$$

The 7 hangs around in front... and we just count up the letters:

$$7x^4w^2$$

Your turn:

Simplify $8aaabccccc$

$8A^3bc^5$

FOR MORE ALGEBRA PRACTICE PROBLEMS, CHECK OUT MY

Algebra Crunchers

Generate an endless number of algebra problems --
with hints and answers, so you can check your work!

Coolmath.com/crunchers

Exponents - Remember These?

Exponent Rules - Rule #1

Can we add these guys?
$$x^2 + x^3$$

No way, dude! Not like terms!

So... can we multiply them?
$$x^2 \cdot x^3$$

Totally! Just write out what each one means and see what happens!

$$x^2 \cdot x^3 = \underbrace{x \cdot x \cdot x \cdot x \cdot x}_{5 \text{ of them}} = x^5$$

That wasn't bad.
What about this guy?
$$w^3 \cdot w^4$$

$$w^3 \cdot w^4 = w \cdot w \cdot w \cdot w \cdot w \cdot w \cdot w = w^7$$

Try it:

base → $y \cdot y^6 \quad y^7$

this 4 stands for one

OK, now do this one:

$$x^{43} \cdot x^{106}$$

$$\begin{array}{r}106\\+43\\\hline 149\end{array}$$

x^{149}

Hey, hey, hey! What -- am I sick or something? Well, yeah, I am. But, that's another story.

Luckily, there is a <u>much</u> easier way to deal with this critter.

Let's look back at the ones we've already done:

$$x^2 \cdot x^3 = x^{2+3} = x^5$$

$$w^3 \cdot w^4 = w^{3+4} = w^7$$

one letter for one $\quad y \cdot y^6 = y^1 \cdot y^6 = y^{1+6} = y^7$

See why it works? If you <u>understand</u> this thing, then you'll always know when you can use it -- <u>and</u> when you can't!

Here's the official rule:

$$\boxed{a^n \cdot a^m = a^{n+m}}$$

Try it:

$$x^{43} \cdot x^{106} \qquad x^{149}$$

Exponent Rules - Rule #1

A couple of things about when you can't use this:

$$w^3 + w^4$$

↑ This is addition -- **not** multiplication!
And these are **not** like terms!

$$x^5 \cdot y^4$$

↑ ↗ The bottom guys (called bases) don't match!

So, there's nothing we can do with either of these.

Here's a fun one!

Let's simplify this: $5xy^3w^2x^4y^{10}w^6$

$= 5\,x^1 x^4\, y^3 y^{10}\, w^2 w^6 = 5 x^{1+4} y^{3+10} w^{2+6}$

↗ just a little commuting!

$= 5x^5 y^{13} w^8$

Your turn:

Simplify: $6x^2yw^4x^5x^2y^8w^9y$

$6x^9 y^{10} w^{13}$

---

40   EXPONENTS AND RADICALS   40

Exponent Rules - Rule #2

What if we divide x^5 by x^2?

$$\frac{x^5}{x^2}$$

There **is** a rule for this, but, it's <u>way</u> better to understand what's going on than to just try to crunch the rule.

Let's write out what each one means:

$$\frac{x^5}{x^2} = \frac{xxxxx}{xx}$$

Remember that $\frac{x}{x} = 1$ ... Just like $\frac{3}{3} = 1$ ...

So, we can cancel some 1's:

$$\frac{x^5}{x^2} = \frac{\cancel{x}\cancel{x}xxx}{\cancel{x}\cancel{x}} = \frac{xxx}{1} = x^3$$

Try it:

Reduce $\frac{y^8}{y^3}$ by writing out what each one means:

y^5

Here's one where using the rule (which I haven't shown you yet) can get tricky:

$$\frac{w^3}{w^5}$$

Let's reason it out:

$$\frac{w^3}{w^5} = \frac{www}{wwwww} = \frac{\cancel{w}\cancel{w}\cancel{w}}{\cancel{w}\cancel{w}\cancel{w}ww} = \frac{1}{ww} = \frac{1}{w^2}$$

Your turn:

Reduce $\dfrac{x}{x^4}$ by writing out what each one means:

$$\frac{\cancel{x}}{\cancel{x}xxx} \quad \frac{1}{x^3}$$

Now, you know enough to reason through some messier ones! (Yes, even without the rule!)

$$\frac{21 x^5 w^3}{9 x^2 w^{10}}$$

I'll walk you through it -- then, you'll be able to do these in one shot.

---

42 EXPONENTS AND RADICALS 42

$$\frac{21x^5w^3}{9x^2w^{10}}$$

① This is just $\frac{21}{9}$ which reduces to $\frac{7}{3}$

$$\frac{7x^5w^3}{3x^2w^{10}}$$

② Five x's on the top...
Two x's on the bottom...
Leaves three x's on the top.

$$\frac{7x^3w^3}{3w^{10}}$$

③ Three w's on the top...
Ten w's on the bottom... Three will cancel top & bottom leaving seven x's on the bottom.

$$\frac{7x^3}{w^7}$$

Done!

Exponent Rules — Rule #2

Try it:

Reduce (sometimes they'll say "simplify.")

$$\frac{12x^6wz^3}{44x^4w^2z^{11}} \quad \frac{3x^2}{11wz^8}$$

Note! at top
$$\frac{\cancel{xxxxxx}}{\cancel{xxxx}} \quad \frac{\cancel{w}w}{\cancel{ww}} \text{ at bottom} \quad \frac{\cancel{zzz}zzzzzzzz}{\cancel{zzz}} \text{ at the bottom}$$

What happens if everyone on the top cancels out?

Let's see...

$$\frac{2x^3w^9}{8x^4w^{20}} = \frac{1}{4xw^{11}} \quad \leftarrow \text{We leave a 1 as a placeholder.}$$

Your turn:

Simplify $\dfrac{5x^{10}z^4w}{10x^{20}z^6w^9} \quad \dfrac{1}{2x^{10}z^2w^8}$

OK, here's the official rule:

$$\boxed{\frac{a^n}{a^m} = a^{n-m}}$$

Let's try it with the first few guys we did:

$$\frac{x^5}{x^2} = x^{5-2} = x^3$$

$$\frac{y^8}{y^3} = y^{8-3} = y^5$$

So far, no problem!
What about this guy? *(when the numerator exponent is less than the denominator exponent, the exponent will be negative)*

$$\frac{w^3}{w^5} = w^{3-5} = w^{-2}$$

Ouch!

I haven't even told you about negative exponents yet... And, even when I do, they're something we'll want to avoid.

So, do these critters with your brain, not the rule!

Exponent Rules - Rule #2

Exponent Rules - Rule #3

What does this thing mean?

$$(x^2)^3$$

Well... 5^3 means $5 \cdot 5 \cdot 5$...

So, $(blob)^3$ means $(blob) \cdot (blob) \cdot (blob)$.

Two ways to look at this thing -- pick your favorite to understand:

WAY 1:

$$(x^2)^3 = x^2 \cdot \underbrace{x^2 \cdot x^2}_{} = x^{2+2+2} = x^6$$

Using exponent rule 1

WAY 2:

$$(x^2)^3 = (xx)^3 = (xx) \cdot (xx)(xx)$$
$$= xxxxxx = x^6$$

Try it:

Simplify $(w^3)^3$ by expanding it out: *this 3·3*

w^9

Do you see a short-cut we can do with the exponents?

Check it out:

$$(x^2)^3 = x^{2 \cdot 3} = x^6$$

$$(w^3)^3 = w^{3 \cdot 3} = w^9$$

Here's the official rule:

$$\boxed{(a^n)^m = a^{n \cdot m}}$$

We can do messier ones too!

$$6(x^4)^7 (w^2)^{10} (y^3)^9 = 6 x^{28} w^{20} y^{27}$$

$x^{28} \quad w^{20} \quad y^{27}$

Try it:

Simplify $2(w^4)^{11} (x^9)^2 (z^3)^{10}$

$2 w^{44} x^{18} z^{30}$

Exponent Rules - Rule #3

Exponent Rules - Rule #4

Don't worry, there are only eight more rules. Heh -- just kidding. This is the last one... and it's really just a notation trick.

$$w^{-3} \quad \text{can be rewritten as} \quad \frac{1}{w^3}$$

$$\frac{1}{x^{-2}} \quad \text{can be rewritten as} \quad x^2$$

This is a trick that works just for negative exponents!

Let's look at these as fractions...

$$\frac{w^{-3}}{1} = \frac{1}{w^3} \quad \text{and} \quad \frac{1}{x^{-2}} = \frac{x^2}{1}$$

Any time a guy with a negative exponent gets moved over the fraction line, the sign turns positive.

Here are the official rules:

$$\boxed{\frac{1}{a^{-n}} = a^n} \quad \text{and} \quad \boxed{a^{-n} = \frac{1}{a^n}}$$

EXPONENTS AND RADICALS

Why do we need these rules? Let's go back to an old example from rule 2:

$$\frac{w^3}{w^5} = w^{3-5} = w^{-2} = \frac{1}{w^2}$$

Look at this carefully... It makes sense, doesn't it? The problem was that the -2 exponent was confusing... so, we need a way to deal with it.

Check out an example with just numbers:

$$2^{-3} = \boxed{\frac{1}{2^3}} = \frac{1}{8} \quad 2 \cdot 2 \cdot 2 = 8$$

when you change the position its positive

Try it: $\frac{\frac{1}{27}}{81}$ $3 \cdot 3 \cdot 3 \cdot 3$

$$3^{-4} = \underline{81} \qquad 4^{-1} = \underline{\frac{1}{4}} \qquad \frac{1}{5^{-2}} = \underline{25} \quad 5 \cdot 5$$

One of the games we'll be playing is to rewrite things so that there are no negative exponents. Check it out:

$$\frac{-2}{w^{-3}} = -2w^3$$

This negative is not effected!

Exponent Rules - Rule #4

Here's another one:

$$\frac{-3x^{-2}w^4}{12z^{-1}} = \frac{-w^4 z}{4x^2}$$

Your turn: *always exchange position on negative exponents in a fraction.*

Rewrite this with no negative exponents:

$$\frac{10a^5 b^{-3} c^{-1}}{25 d^{-4} e^6} \qquad \frac{2a^5 d^4}{5 b^3 e^6 c} \quad \text{correct the 1st try}$$

Now, here's a big rule in math -- all teachers, all books and all tests follow it:

> **Never leave negative exponents in your answers!**

Exponent Rules – Putting Rules #1-4 Together

Here are our rules:

$$a^n a^m = a^{n+m}$$

add exponents together only

$$\frac{a^n}{a^m} = a^{n-m} \quad \text{numerator} \atop \text{denominator}$$

subtract the denominator exponents from the numerator

$$(a^n)^m = a^{n \cdot m}$$

multiply exponents

$$\frac{1}{a^{-n}} = a^n \qquad a^{-n} = \frac{1}{a^n}$$

Rewrite negative exponents invert them always

Now, we can do problems that use more than one of these. Exciting, isn't it?

Check it out:

Let's simplify this guy:

$$2(x^2)^4 (w^3)^6 (x^7)^2 w$$
$$= 2 x^{2 \cdot 4} w^{3 \cdot 6} x^{7 \cdot 2} w = 2 x^8 x^{14} w^{18} w^1$$
$$= 2 x^{8+14} w^{18+1} = 2 x^{22} w^{19}$$

Try it:

Simplify $5x^2 w^4 z (x^3)^6 (w^2)^4 (z^5)^2$

$5x^{20} w^{12} z^{11}$

Here's another one:

Let's simplify this:

$$\frac{-4(x^2)^7 (w^8)^3}{22 x^6 (w^{10})^3 z} = \frac{-2 x^{14} w^{24}}{11 x^6 w^{30} z} = \frac{-2x^8}{11 w^6 z}$$

Your turn:

Simplify $\dfrac{9 x^{10} (w^3)^2 (z^2)^{11}}{39 (x^4)^5 w^{10} (z^8)^4}$

$\dfrac{3 x^{10} w^6 z^{22}}{13 x^{20} w^{10} z^{32}} \quad \dfrac{3}{13 x^{10} w^4 z^{10}}$

One more:

$$\frac{18 x^{-3} (w^2)^4 z^{-1}}{10 x^{-1} w^{-5} z^{11}} = \frac{9 x^1 w^8 w^5}{5 x^3 z^{11} z^1} = \frac{9 w^{13}}{5 x^2 z^{12}}$$

* I deal with the negative exponents first!

EXPONENTS AND RADICALS

Try it:

Simplify $\dfrac{-2(x^3)^7 w^{-9} z^{-2}}{12 x^{-8} w (z^2)^{-3}}$ $\begin{matrix}2\cdot 2\cdot 2 = 8\\ \text{here}\end{matrix}$

$\dfrac{-x^{21} \cdot x^8}{6 \quad w+w^9 \quad z^2 + z^8} \quad ; \quad \dfrac{-x^{29}}{6 w^{10} z^{10}}$

FOR MORE ALGEBRA PRACTICE PROBLEMS, CHECK OUT MY

Algebra Crunchers

Generate an endless number of algebra problems --
with hints and answers, so you can check your work!

Coolmath.com/crunchers

Exponent Rules - Review

You should know these rules cold!

$$a^n a^m = a^{n+m}$$

example:

$$y^5 y^3 = y^{5+3} = y^8$$

Try it:

$$x^2 x^4$$

Now, explain why this rule works!

$$\frac{a^n}{a^m} = a^{n-m}$$

example:

$$\frac{x^7}{x^3} = \frac{xxxxxxx}{xxx} = x^4$$

EXPONENTS AND RADICALS

example:

$$\frac{w}{w^3} = \frac{w}{www} = \frac{1}{w^2}$$

Now that you remember this, you don't have to write it out.

Try it:

$$\frac{x^2}{x^8}$$

$$\boxed{(a^n)^m = a^{n \cdot m}}$$

example:

$$(y^5)^3 = y^{5 \cdot 3} = y^{15}$$

Your turn:

$$(x^2)^3$$

Now, explain why this rule works!

Exponent Rules - Review

$$\boxed{\dfrac{1}{a^{-n}} = a^n}$$

example:

$$\dfrac{1}{3^{-4}} = 3^4 = 81$$

example:

$$\dfrac{1}{x^{-2}} = x^2$$

example:

$$\dfrac{-2}{3w^{-5}} = \dfrac{-2w^5}{3}$$

Try it:

$$\dfrac{1}{6x^{-3}}$$

$$\boxed{a^{-n} = \dfrac{1}{a^n}}$$

example:

$$x^{-3} = \dfrac{1}{x^3}$$

example:

$$2 \cdot 3^{-2} w^{-4} = \dfrac{2}{9w^4}$$

Try it:

$$6x^{-4}$$

Write all the rules here ↓

Exponent Rules - Review

Exponent Rules - Rule #5

What does this thing mean?

$$(xy)^4$$

It's 4 blobs of (xy) all multiplied together:

$$(xy)^4 = (xy)(xy)(xy)(xy)$$
$$= xyxyxyxy$$
commute $\rightarrow$ $= xxxxyyyy$
$$= x^4 y^4$$

We can cut to the chase and, kind of, distribute the exponent into each guy:

$$(xy)^4 = x^4 y^4$$

Here's the general rule:

$$\boxed{(ab)^n = a^n b^n}$$

Try it:

$$(wz)^3$$

Explain why this works!

Check out another example:

Rewrite $(6a^2bc^4)^3$

$$(6a^2bc^4)^3 = (6)^3(a^2)^3(b)^3(c^4)^3$$
$$= 216\,a^6b^3c^{12}$$

∗ The old rules will pop up in these too!

Your turn:

$$(-4xy^5z^3)^2$$

BUT, BEWARE!

You can get into a lot of trouble if you get carried away with this rule!

Look at this guy:

$$(x+y)^2$$

Remember what it means? Can we do this?

$$(x+y)^2 \stackrel{?}{=} x^2 + y^2$$

BUZZZZZZZ! No way, Dude!

What does it really mean?

Exponent Rules - Rule #5

$$(x+y)^2 = (x+y)(x+y)$$
$$= x^2 + xy + xy + y^2$$
$$= x^2 + 2xy + y^2$$

↗ This is definitely <u>not</u> $x^2 + y^2$!

Take a close look at what's different here:

$$(xy)^2 \qquad\qquad (x+y)^2$$

↗ These are being multiplied -- We can use the rule:

$$(xy)^2 = x^2 y^2$$

↗ These are being added -- we <u>can't</u> use the rule!

EXPONENTS AND RADICALS

Exponent Rules - Rule #6

Check out what this guy means:

$$\left(\frac{x}{y}\right)^5$$

That's 5 blobs of $\left(\frac{x}{y}\right)$ all multiplied together:

$$\left(\frac{x}{y}\right)^5 = \left(\frac{x}{y}\right)\left(\frac{x}{y}\right)\left(\frac{x}{y}\right)\left(\frac{x}{y}\right)\left(\frac{x}{y}\right)$$

$$= \frac{x}{y} \cdot \frac{x}{y} \cdot \frac{x}{y} \cdot \frac{x}{y} \cdot \frac{x}{y}$$

$$= \frac{x \cdot x \cdot x \cdot x \cdot x}{y \cdot y \cdot y \cdot y \cdot y} = \frac{x^5}{y^5}$$

It's like the exponent is getting distributed to the top and the bottom!

$$\left(\frac{x}{y}\right)^5 = \frac{x^5}{y^5}$$

Here's the general rule:

$$\boxed{\left(\frac{a}{b}\right)^n = \frac{a^n}{b^n}}$$

Try it:
$$\left(\frac{w}{z}\right)^3$$

Explain why this rule works:

Here's a messier one...
We're going to need our old rules too!
Let's rewrite this guy:
$$\left(\frac{xw^3}{-5z^4}\right)^2$$

We just hammer away at the rules a little at a time...

$$\left(\frac{xw^3}{-5z^4}\right)^2 = \frac{(xw^3)^2}{(-5z^4)^2} = \frac{(x)^2(w^3)^2}{(-5)^2(z^4)^2}$$

$$= \frac{x^2 w^6}{25 z^8} \quad \text{done!}$$

Your turn:
Simplify $\left(\dfrac{3a^5 b^2}{2c}\right)^4$

Simplify $\left(\dfrac{16 x^{-2} w^3 z^4}{6 x^{-5} w z^{-2}}\right)^3$

* clean up the inside first!

Exponent Rules – Rule #6

Radicals - A Review of Radicals

SQUARE ROOTS:

Here are a few:

$$\sqrt{4} = 2 \qquad \sqrt{100} = 10 \qquad \sqrt{7} \approx 2.6457...$$

The first two popped cleanly (because they had perfect squares inside.) But, the last guy didn't. He's an irrational number. His decimal part goes on forever and ever and never repeats.

$$\sqrt{7} \approx 2.6457...$$

Just like π! The reason I used "$\approx$" instead of a regular "$=$" is because I can't really write the exact number down.

$$\approx \text{ means approximately } =$$

When roots like $\sqrt{7}$ don't pop cleanly, in math, we just leave them as radicals. It's more accurate this way!

So... $\sqrt{5}$? Just leave it as $\sqrt{5}$! Done!

We cannot do square roots like this yet:

$$\sqrt{-25}$$

↑ The negative is a problem.

EXPONENTS AND RADICALS

There *is* an answer for this guy, but you'll learn about it later.

Try it:

$$\sqrt{9} \qquad \sqrt{37} \qquad \sqrt{-16}$$

CUBE ROOTS:

Here are a few:

$$\sqrt[3]{8} = 2 \qquad \sqrt[3]{1} = 1 \qquad \sqrt[3]{-64} = -4$$

OK... So, how am I figuring these out? Pretty easy.

If I want $\sqrt[3]{27}$, I ask myself

"What number cubed gives me 27?"
$$(\quad)^3$$

$$(3)^3 = 27 \longrightarrow \sqrt[3]{27} = 3$$

Here's a trickier one:

$$\sqrt[3]{-8} = ?$$

Hey -- that inside guy is negative! Are we allowed to do this? We sure couldn't do square roots of negative guys.

Let's think about it...

Radicals - A Review of Radicals

Can we find a number that goes in this?

$$()^3 = -8$$

Yepperooski!

$$(-2)^3 = (-2)(-2)(-2) = -8$$

so $\sqrt[3]{-8} = -2$

Now that we're thinking like this, let's go back and look at square roots...

$$\sqrt{36} = ?$$

Can we find a number that goes in here?

$$()^2 = ()() = 36$$

$$(6)^2 = (6)(6) = 36$$

so $\sqrt{36} = 6$

By the way, this thing is really

$$\sqrt[2]{36} = 6$$

But, square roots are so commonly used, that we just leave off the 2 and assume it's there.

EXPONENTS AND RADICALS

What about $\sqrt{-49}$?

Can we find a number that goes in this?

$$(\ )^2 = (\ )(\ ) = -49$$

Since these are the same number, we'd either have

$$(-)(-) = + \quad \text{or} \quad (+)(+) = +$$

$$(\ )^2 = -49$$

That's why a square can't be negative!

In fact, this goes for all even roots.

$$\sqrt[4]{-16} \quad \leftarrow \text{can't do!}$$

Since no number works in

$$(\ )^4 = -16$$

There'd be an even number of the guy multiplied together:

$$(\ )(\ )(\ )(\ ) = -16$$
$$(-)(-)(-)(-) = +$$
$$(+)(+)(+)(+) = +$$

This negative can't happen!

Try it:

$\sqrt{-1} =$ ___ $\sqrt{1} =$ ___ $\sqrt[3]{0} =$ ___

$\sqrt[3]{-64} =$ ___ $\sqrt[4]{81} =$ ___ $\sqrt{81} =$ ___

$\sqrt{-4} =$ ___

OK, now here's something math people can get really picky about:

$$\sqrt{x^2} = ?$$

What goes in here?

$$(\ )^2 = (\ )(\ ) = x^2$$

Is it just x?

The answer is... sometimes.
Check it out:

What if x = 3?

$$\sqrt{(3)^2} = \sqrt{9} = 3$$

Yeah-- that works.

What if x = -3?

$$\sqrt{(-3)^2} = \sqrt{9} = 3$$

Not the same!

So, it doesn't work when x is negative!

EXPONENTS AND RADICALS

Technically,
$$\sqrt{x^2} = x \text{ only when } x \geq 0$$

If $x < 0$, we'd say
$$\sqrt{x^2} = |x|$$

Look again at our example:
$$\sqrt{(-3)^2} = |-3| = 3$$

Radicals - Rules for Radicals

Here's the first rule:

$$\boxed{\sqrt[n]{a}\,\sqrt[n]{b} = \sqrt[n]{ab}}$$

*Note that the types of root (n) have to match!

Here are a few examples:

$\sqrt{2}\,\sqrt{8} = \sqrt{2\cdot 8} = \sqrt{16} = 4$

↑ Pop these into your calculator to check!

$\sqrt[3]{2}\,\sqrt[3]{4} = \sqrt[3]{2\cdot 4} = \sqrt[3]{8} = 2$

$\sqrt{5}\,\sqrt{7} = \sqrt{5\cdot 7} = \sqrt{35}$ ← can't pop

---

$\sqrt{3}\,\sqrt{3} = \sqrt{3\cdot 3} = \sqrt{9} = 3$

$2\sqrt{2} \cdot 3\sqrt{50}$ Do a little commuting...

$= 2\cdot 3 \cdot \sqrt{2}\,\sqrt{50} = 6\sqrt{2\cdot 50} = 6\sqrt{100}$

$= 6\cdot 10 = 60$

(If you don't believe me, grab a calculator & check!)

Your turn:

$\sqrt[4]{3}\,\sqrt[4]{27}$

EXPONENTS AND RADICALS

$$\sqrt{6}\sqrt{6}$$

$$\sqrt{8}\ \sqrt[3]{2}$$

$$5\sqrt{2} \cdot 8\sqrt{18}$$

Here's the second rule:

$$\boxed{\dfrac{\sqrt[n]{a}}{\sqrt[n]{b}} = \sqrt[n]{\dfrac{a}{b}}}$$

* Note again that the types of roots need to match!

Here are a few examples:

$$\dfrac{\sqrt{32}}{\sqrt{2}} = \sqrt{\dfrac{32}{2}} = \sqrt{16} = 4 \quad \text{check it on your calculator!}$$

$$\dfrac{\sqrt[3]{3}}{\sqrt[3]{81}} = \sqrt[3]{\dfrac{3}{81}} = \sqrt[3]{\dfrac{1}{27}} = \dfrac{\sqrt[3]{1}}{\sqrt[3]{27}} = \dfrac{1}{3}$$

(we used the rule twice here!)

$$\dfrac{\sqrt{52}}{\sqrt[3]{2}} \quad \text{roots don't match!}$$

$$\frac{12\sqrt{32}}{2\sqrt{8}} = \frac{12}{2}\sqrt{\frac{32}{8}} = 6\sqrt{4} = 6 \cdot 2 = 12$$

Your turn:

$$\frac{\sqrt{2}}{\sqrt{200}}$$

$$\frac{\sqrt[3]{500}}{\sqrt[3]{4}}$$

$$\frac{15\sqrt{75}}{5\sqrt{3}}$$

Radicals - Rewriting Radicals

There are lots of things in math that aren't really necessary anymore. These date back to the days (daze) before calculators. Lucky for us, we still get to do them! Once something makes its way into a math text, it won't leave! (much like a fungus or a bad house guest.)

So, let's go back -- way back -- to the days before calculators -- way back -- to 1970! There were no VCRs, no cell phones, no answering machines, dinosaurs ruled the earth! I had to walk 3 miles to school in knee-deep snow... uphill... both ways! It was awful! (sniff)

Anyway, before calculators, math geeks had to crunch out decimals for things like

$$\frac{318672}{5931}$$

by hand using long division! (Yuck.)

They had tables that listed decimal values for radicals:

Table 1 Powers and roots

n	n^2	$\sqrt{n}$	n^3	$\sqrt[3]{n}$
1	1	1.000	1	1.000
2	4	1.414	8	1.260
3	9	1.732	27	1.442
4	16	2.000	64	1.587
5	25	2.236	125	1.710
6	36	2.449	216	1.817
7	49	2.646	343	1.913
8	64	2.828	512	2.000
9	81	3.000	729	2.080

And they had some basic guys memorized like
$$\sqrt{2} \approx 1.414$$
So, if they needed a decimal value for a guy like
$$7\sqrt{2}$$
they'd put in the memorized 1.414 part and crunch it out by hand:

$$7\sqrt{2} \approx 7(1.414) \rightarrow$$

```
  1.414
×     7
───────
  9.898
```

Not very accurate either.
My calculator says
$$7\sqrt{2} \approx 9.89949...$$

So... what if they needed to crunch this guy?
$$5\sqrt{200}$$

Well... $\sqrt{200}$ might be too big for the tables and, even though they were geeks, I'm sure they couldn't have memorized <u>all</u> the radicals.

So, what did they do?

They rewrote the radical so that the smallest number possible was inside the radical.

EXPONENTS AND RADICALS

Check it out:

$$5\sqrt{200} = 5\sqrt{100 \cdot 2} = 5\sqrt{100}\sqrt{2} = 5 \cdot 10\sqrt{2}$$

Rule from last section

$$= 50\sqrt{2}$$

Now, since they knew that $\sqrt{2} \approx 1.414$, they could pop a fairly accurate decimal. But, we're going to just leave it in its pure form since it's more accurate this way!

What we're really doing when we try to rewrite these things is that we are going on a perfect square hunt!

Look at this guy:

$$\sqrt{75}$$

See any perfect squares hiding in here? What about 25?

$$\sqrt{75} = \sqrt{25 \cdot 3} = \sqrt{25}\sqrt{3} = 5\sqrt{3}$$

Try it:

Rewrite $\sqrt{45}$ so that the smallest number possible is inside the radical.

Radicals - Rewriting Radicals

Here's a trickier one:
$$\sqrt{588}$$
There are two perfect squares hiding in here... We'll need to completely factor this thing to find them.

$$\sqrt{588} = \sqrt{4 \cdot 49 \cdot 3} = \sqrt{4}\sqrt{49}\sqrt{3} = 2 \cdot 7\sqrt{3} = 14\sqrt{3}$$

(You can check to see if this is right by popping $\sqrt{588}$ and $14\sqrt{3}$ into your calculator. You should get the same thing.)

Try it:

Rewrite $\sqrt{1575}$ so that the smallest number possible is inside the radical.

You can do this with other kinds of roots too -- like cube roots.

Check it out:

We'll be on a perfect cube hunt this time!

$$\sqrt[3]{56} = \sqrt[3]{8 \cdot 7} = \sqrt[3]{8}\sqrt[3]{7} = 2\sqrt[3]{7}$$

Try it:

$$\sqrt[3]{54}$$

By the way, on typical math tests and in typical math books, they call this stuff "simplifying" or "reducing" radicals.

But, I ask you... which is "simpler?"

$$\sqrt{200} \quad \text{or} \quad 10\sqrt{2}$$

Which would take less time to punch into a calculator?

$$\sqrt{200}$$

If I had my way (which I rarely do), I'd bag this process altogether. But, it's in all the books and it will be on most algebra tests you'll run into.

So, let's just think of it as a game we need to play.

Radicals - Rewriting Radicals

Radicals - Adding & Subtracting Radicals

This game goes along with the game in the last section. Yes, it's definitely a pre-calculator thing... But, it's on a lot of standardized math tests... So, here we go!

We want to add these guys without using decimals:

$$\sqrt{2} + \sqrt{8}$$

The game is to simplify everyone and see if we can combine anything.

$\sqrt{2}$ is done already.

$$\sqrt{8} = \sqrt{4 \cdot 2} = \sqrt{4}\sqrt{2} = 2\sqrt{2}$$

So, $\sqrt{2} + \sqrt{8} = \sqrt{2} + 2\sqrt{2}$

Now, we treat the radicals like variables. Think of it as

$$y + 2y = 3y$$

$$\sqrt{2} + \sqrt{8} = \sqrt{2} + 2\sqrt{2} = 3\sqrt{2}$$
done!

Here's another one:

$$\sqrt{48} - \sqrt{3} + \sqrt{75}$$

Rewrite the radicals...

$$\sqrt{48} - \sqrt{3} + \sqrt{75} = \sqrt{16 \cdot 3} - \sqrt{3} + \sqrt{25 \cdot 3}$$

$$= 4\sqrt{3} - \sqrt{3} + 5\sqrt{3} = 8\sqrt{3}$$

(like $4x - x + 5x = 8x$)

Your turn:

$$\sqrt{45} + \sqrt{20} + \sqrt{5} - \sqrt{125}$$

FOR MORE ALGEBRA PRACTICE PROBLEMS, CHECK OUT MY

Algebra Crunchers

Generate an endless number of algebra problems -- with hints and answers, so you can check your work!

Coolmath.com/crunchers

Radicals - Adding & Subtracting Radicals

Radicals - Multiplying Messier Radicals

We're going to need this for the next section. We'll need to FOIL guys like

$$(5-\sqrt{2})(5+\sqrt{2})$$

The FOIL part works the same as always -- we just have to deal with the radicals. Let's go!

$$(5-\sqrt{2})(5+\sqrt{2}) = \underset{F}{(5)(5)} + \underset{O}{5\sqrt{2}} - \underset{I}{5\sqrt{2}} - \underset{L}{\sqrt{2}\sqrt{2}}$$

$$= 25 - \sqrt{2 \cdot 2} = 25 - \sqrt{4}$$

$$= 25 - 2 = 23$$

Try it:

$$(3+\sqrt{7})(3-\sqrt{7})$$

Radicals - Rationalizing Denominators

Let's fly back again to the days of dinosaurs and no calculators!

If math geeks had to calculate a decimal for something like

$$\frac{3}{\sqrt{2}}$$

things got really ugly. They'd have to use a table to get the value for $\sqrt{2}$ ... then, they'd have to do the long division by hand:

$$\sqrt{2} \approx 1.414 \quad \rightarrow \quad 1.414 \overline{)3.000}$$

Yuck!

So, it was a <u>lot</u> easier for them if there wasn't a radical in the denominator.

They created a fun little game called rationalizing the denominator.

Here's how it goes:

$$\frac{3}{\sqrt{2}} = \frac{3}{\sqrt{2}} \cdot \frac{\sqrt{2}}{\sqrt{2}} = \frac{3\sqrt{2}}{\sqrt{2}\sqrt{2}} = \frac{3\sqrt{2}}{\sqrt{4}} = \frac{3\sqrt{2}}{2}$$

↑ Multiply by a magic 1.

Here's another one:

$$\frac{5}{\sqrt{10}}$$

$$\frac{5}{\sqrt{10}} = \frac{5}{\sqrt{10}} \cdot \frac{\sqrt{10}}{\sqrt{10}} = \frac{5\sqrt{10}}{\sqrt{100}} = \frac{5\sqrt{10}}{10} = \frac{\sqrt{10}}{2}$$

Reduce: $\frac{5}{10} = \frac{1}{2}$

Your turn:

Rationalize the denominator:

$$\frac{6}{\sqrt{15}}$$

They get messier:
What if we needed to get the radical out of this denominator?

$$\frac{5}{2-\sqrt{3}}$$

Same game -- we still multiply by a magic 1...

$$\frac{5}{2-\sqrt{3}}$$

The magic 1 will be made up of this guy's conjugate. Well now, that was helpful, wasn't it?

Conjugate = same guy, different sign

EXPONENTS AND RADICALS

So, the conjugate of $2-\sqrt{3}$ is $2+\sqrt{3}$.

Check out how it works:

$$\frac{5}{2-\sqrt{3}} \cdot \frac{2+\sqrt{3}}{2+\sqrt{3}} = \frac{5}{(2-\sqrt{3})} \cdot \frac{(2+\sqrt{3})}{(2+\sqrt{3})}$$

Put ( ) around everyone or you're really going to mess things up!

distribute

$$\frac{5}{(2-\sqrt{3})} \cdot \frac{(2+\sqrt{3})}{(2+\sqrt{3})} = \frac{10+5\sqrt{3}}{4-\sqrt{9}} = \frac{10+5\sqrt{3}}{4-3}$$

FOIL

$$= 10 + 5\sqrt{3}$$

Not only did we ditch the radical in the denominator, in this one, we ditched the whole denominator.

Here's another one:

$$\frac{4}{1+\sqrt{7}}$$

$$\frac{4}{1+\sqrt{7}} = \frac{4}{(1+\sqrt{7})} \cdot \frac{(1-\sqrt{7})}{(1-\sqrt{7})} = \frac{4-4\sqrt{7}}{1-\sqrt{49}} ...$$

Radicals - Rationalizing Denominators

$$= \frac{4-4\sqrt{7}}{1-7} = \frac{4-4\sqrt{7}}{-6} = \frac{-2(-2+2\sqrt{7})}{-6} = \frac{-2+2\sqrt{7}}{3}$$

Try it:

Rationalize the denominator

$$\frac{3}{2-\sqrt{6}}$$

Radicals - Fractional Exponents

Don't get all freaked out about these -- it's just a different notation for what you've already been doing.

$$\sqrt[3]{8} \text{ can be written as } 8^{1/3}$$

$$\sqrt{15} \text{ can be written as } 15^{1/2}$$

* Remember that $\sqrt{}$ is really $\sqrt[2]{}$ ... we just assume the 2.

Not that bad, is it?

Here's the general rule:

$$\boxed{\sqrt[n]{a} = a^{1/n}}$$

This notation has some advantages because it will help you understand some things better. Check it out:

$$\sqrt{5} \cdot \sqrt{5} = 5^{1/2} \cdot 5^{1/2} = 5^{1/2 + 1/2} = 5^1 = 5$$

Now, we can show why this rule works:

$$\sqrt[n]{a} \sqrt[n]{b} = \sqrt[n]{ab}$$

$$\sqrt[n]{a}\sqrt[n]{b} = a^{1/n}b^{1/n} = (ab)^{1/n} = \sqrt[n]{ab}$$

↑ one of our exponent rules

We can do the same thing with this rule:

$$\frac{\sqrt[n]{a}}{\sqrt[n]{b}} = \sqrt[n]{\frac{a}{b}}$$

$$\frac{\sqrt[n]{a}}{\sqrt[n]{b}} = \frac{a^{1/n}}{b^{1/n}} = \left(\frac{a}{b}\right)^{1/n} = \sqrt[n]{\frac{a}{b}}$$

↑ exponent rule

We can also figure out weird numbers like

$$16^{3/4}$$

Using this rule:

$$\boxed{\left(\sqrt[n]{a}\right)^m = a^{m/n}}$$

The only tricky part this one is to remember how to write the fraction:

$\frac{3}{4}$ ← exponent
← radical

It's alphabetical!

---

86   EXPONENTS AND RADICALS   86

$$16^{3/4} = \sqrt[4]{16^3}$$

By the way, there's kind of a cool way to pop this guy without a calculator. (Hey -- if you're stranded on a desert island and the professor isn't there to make you a calculator out of coconuts and salt water...)

You can rewrite this guy as a 4th power. → $16^{3/4}$

$$16^{3/4} = (2^4)^{3/4} = 2^{4 \cdot 3/4} = 2^3 = 8$$

Eh. Not that useful... But, if you don't have anything to do on a Saturday night...

Try it:

  Pop this without a calculator: $9^{5/2}$

You can use this new notation to help you deal with messy radical problems.

Check it out:

$$\sqrt[4]{\frac{2x^{-1}w^5}{32x^7w}} = \left(\frac{2x^{-1}w^5}{32x^7w}\right)^{1/4} = \left(\frac{w^4}{16x^8}\right)^{1/4}$$

Radicals - Fractional Exponents

$$= \frac{(w^4)^{1/4}}{(16x^8)^{1/4}} = \frac{w}{2x^2}$$

Here's another one:

$$\sqrt[3]{8x^3w^9z^6} = (8x^3w^9z^6)^{1/3}$$
$$= 8^{1/3}(x^3)^{1/3}(w^9)^{1/3}(z^6)^{1/3}$$
$$= 2xw^3z^2$$

Try it:

$$\sqrt[5]{\left(\frac{a^7b^3}{32a^2b^{-7}}\right)^2}$$

$$\sqrt[4]{\left(\frac{81a^5b^{-5}}{ab^3}\right)^3}$$

EXPONENTS AND RADICALS

Freaked out by FRACTIONS?

Then get a quick review at
Coolmath.com/fractions

FOR MORE ALGEBRA PRACTICE PROBLEMS, CHECK OUT MY

Algebra Crunchers

Generate an endless number of algebra problems --
with hints and answers, so you can check your work!

Coolmath.com/crunchers

ARE YOU TOTALLY STRESSED OUT?

You don't have to feel out of control. You don't have to feel nervous. You don't have to feel tired and foggy all the time. Believe me, I've been there myself. I totally remember what it was like to be a student -- and I was a student for a LONG time! Since then, I've been a college teacher so I'm around students all the time - most of them stressed out. Over the years, I've been teaching my students how to de-stress and how to deal with stress... I finally decided to make a stress management site specially designed FOR students -- and anyone else who feels stressed out.

So, settle down and KNOW that you CAN lower your stress! You really ARE in control of what's going on in your world!
YOU CAN ACTUALLY BE HAPPY AND RELAXED -- yeah, even while you're a student!

TotallyStressedOut.com
The stress management site for students

Are you already in credit card trouble?
Is your FICO score the pits?
Uh... FICO who?
Do you want to learn about this stuff?

Do you want to learn how to be SMART & RICH?

financeFREAK.com

A fool and his money are soon parted.
Don't be a fool... Be a FREAK!

POLYNOMIALS
-AND-
FACTORING

Polynomials - Sticking Numbers In

In regular math books, this is usually called "substituting" or "evaluating"... But, those are pretty big words for something so easy. Check it out:

We are given something like this:

$$x^2 - 4x + 1$$

And we need to find what this thing equals when we put a number in for x... Like

$$x = 3$$

Everywhere you see an x... stick in a 3!

$$x^2 - 4x + 1 = (3)^2 - 4(3) + 1 = -2$$

What about $x = -5$?

We need to be careful with this negative! Use ( )!

$$x^2 - 4x + 1 = (-5)^2 - 4(-5) + 1 = 46$$

Try it:

Let $x = 2$:

Let $x = -1$:

Polynomials - What's a Polynomial, Anyway?

That critter in the last section is a polynomial!

$$x^2 - 4x + 1$$

Here are some others:

$$x^2 + 7x - 3$$
$$4a^3 + 7a^2 + a$$
$$nm^2 - m$$
$$3x - 2$$
$$5$$

Polynomial is a pretty big word, but it's not a hard thing. (We use big words in math so other people think we are smart.)

For now (and, probably, forever), you can just think of a polynomial as a bunch of blobs all added or subtracted. The blobs are just products of numbers and letters with exponents. As you'll see later on, polynomials have cool graphs:

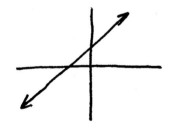 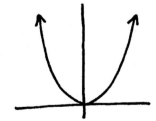 

Polynomials - Some Math Words to Know

Here's a polynomial:

$$2x^3 - 5x^2 + x + 9$$

Each one of the little product-blobs is a "term."

$$2x^3 \quad -5x^2 \quad +x \quad +9$$
$$\uparrow \qquad \uparrow \qquad \uparrow \qquad \uparrow$$
$$\text{term} \quad \text{term} \quad \text{term} \quad \text{term}$$

So, this guy has four terms.

The coefficients are the numbers in front of the letters:

$$2x^3 - 5x^2 + x + 9$$
$$\uparrow \qquad \uparrow \qquad \uparrow \qquad \uparrow$$
$$2 \qquad -5 \qquad 1 \qquad 9$$

Remember $x = 1 \cdot x$

We just pretend this last guy has a letter behind him.

"Poly" means "many."

When there is only one term, it's a <u>mono</u>mial:

$$5x$$

When there are two terms, it's a <u>bi</u>nomial:

$$2x + 3$$

When there are three terms, it's a <u>trinomial</u>:
$$x^2 - x - 6$$

So, what about four terms? Quadnomial? Naw - we don't go there. Too hard to pronounce. This guy is just called a polynomial
$$7x^3 + 5x^2 - 2x + 4$$

There's one more word I need to tell you about:

degree

Here's how you find the degree of a polynomial:
   Look at each of the terms...
   Whoever has the most letters wins!

Check it out:
   This is a 5th degree polynomial:
$$3x^2 - 8x^4 + x^5$$

       This guy has 5 letters...
        The degree is 5.

This is a 7th degree polynomial:

$$6mn^2 + \underbrace{m^3n^4}_{} + 8$$

This guy has 7 letters...
The degree is 7.

This is a 1ST degree polynomial:

$$2x + 7$$

This guy has 1 letter...
The degree is 1.

What about this guy?

$$8$$

How many letters does he have? ZERO!
So, he's a zero degree polynomial.

By the way, the coefficients don't have anything to do with the degree.

Your turn:

Find the degree:

$$3x - x^2 \qquad a^4b - 7a^2b^2 \qquad 7x - 1$$

Polynomials - Some Math Words to Know

Before we go on, I want you to know that Algebra isn't going to be just a bunch of weird words that you don't understand. I just had to start with some words at the beginning so you'd know what the heck I'm talking about!

FOR MORE ALGEBRA PRACTICE PROBLEMS, CHECK OUT MY

Algebra Crunchers

Generate an endless number of algebra problems -- with hints and answers, so you can check your work!

Coolmath.com/crunchers

Polynomials - Adding & Subtracting

The trick to this is to add or subtract things that look alike. It's usually called "combining like terms."

Here's a really basic example:

If you have 3 bears and someone gives you 2 more bears, how many bears do you have?

$$3 🐻 + 2 🐻 = 5 🐻$$

5 bears!

Now, what if you have one bear and 4 cats and someone gives you 6 bears, 2 cats and 3 dogs? What do you have?

$$(🐻 + 4 🐱) + (6 🐻 + 2 🐱 + 3 🐶)$$
$$= 7 🐻 + 6 🐱 + 3 🐶$$

7 bears, 6 cats, and 3 really stupid looking dogs.

Get it? Now we can do this:

$$(b + 4c) + (6b + 2c + 3d) = 7b + 6c + 3d$$

Here's what's really going on:

$$(b + 4c) + (6b + 2c + 3d)$$

We gather up the like terms...

$$= (b + 6b) + (4c + 2c) + 3d$$

↑ This guy didn't have a partner.

And add the coefficients...

$$= 7b + 6c + 3d \quad \text{done!}$$

Try it:

You have 4 bunnies, 2 piggies and 6 horsies... just kidding!

$$(3x - 4w + z) + (6x + 2w + 5z)$$

Now, look at this guy:

$$3x^2 - 5x + 7$$

There's an x^2 guy. There's an x guy. There's a regular number guy.

POLYNOMIALS, FACTORING AND DIVISION

So, if we wanted to add these two polys...

$$3x^2 - 5x + 7 \text{ and } x^2 + 2x - 1$$

We just add the guys that match up!

$(3x^2 - 5x + 7) + (x^2 + 2x - 1)$

$= (3x^2 + x^2) + (-5x + 2x) + (7-1) = 4x^2 - 3x + 6$

Your turn:

$(8x^2 - x + 3) + (2x^2 + 6x + 1)$

Here's a messier one:

$(6nm^2 + 7n - 6m + 3) + (2nm^2 + 8m - 2)$

Who matches up?

$= (6nm^2 + 2nm^2) + 7n + (-6m + 8m) + (3-2)$
$\qquad\qquad\qquad\qquad\uparrow$
$\qquad\qquad\qquad\text{No partner}$

$= 8nm^2 + 7n + 2m + 1$

Try it:

$(4a^2b - ab + 3b^2 - 1) + (a^2b + 8ab - 6a^2 + 5)$

Polynomials – Adding & Subtracting

Subtracting works the same way -- you just really have to be careful with the minus! Check it out:

$$(5x^2+3x-6)-(3x^2-x+5)$$

This guy distributes in to these!

$$= 5x^2+3x-6-3x^2+x-5$$
$$= (5x^2-3x^2)+(3x+x)+(-6-5)$$
$$= 2x^2+4x-11$$

And, no, you don't have to write out all these steps once you get good at these. I'm just showing a bunch of steps so you can follow it.

Your turn:

$$(3x^2-4x+8)-(x^2+7x-5)$$

Before I do the next one, do this for me:

Subtract 3 from 5.

I hope you did this: $5 - 3 = 2$

So, I hope you won't mess up the set-up on this guy:

   Subtract $2a^3 + b - 3$ from $8a^3 + b + 4$.

Be careful with the wording!

$(8a^3 + b + 4) - (2a^3 + b - 3)$

$= (8a^3 - 2a^3) + (b - b) + (4 + 3) = 6a^3 + 7$

Your turn:

   Subtract $3x^2 - 6xy + y^2$ from $x^2 - 4xy + 5y^2$.

Polynomials - Multiplying Easy Ones

Remember the distributive property?

$$a(b+c) = ab + ac$$

Check it with this easy example:

$$2(4+5) = 2 \cdot 4 + 2 \cdot 5$$
$$2 \cdot 9 = 8 + 10$$
$$18 = 18 \quad \text{Yep -- it works!}$$

Now, we'll be doing it with x critters.
Let's multiply this:

$$3x^2(x+5)$$

$$3x^2(x+5) = 3x^2(x) + 3x^2(5)$$
$$= 3x^2 x^1 + 3 \cdot 5 x^2 = 3x^3 + 15x^2$$

Try it:

$$6x^4(2x^2+3)$$

POLYNOMIALS, FACTORING AND DIVISION

Here's another one:

$$4w^6(3w^2 + w - 1)$$
$$= 4w^6(3w^2) + 4w^6(w) - 4w^6(1)$$
$$= 4\cdot 3 w^6 w^2 + 4w^6 w^1 - 4w^6 = 12w^8 + 4w^7 - 4w^6$$

Your turn:

$$10x^3(2x^5 + 1 - 3x^2 + x)$$

Here's a harder one -- we'll have two letters to keep track of:

$$2xy^3(3 - x^2 + 7xy^5 + y) =$$
$$2xy^3(3) - 2xy^3(x^2) + 2xy^3(7xy^5) + 2xy^3(y)$$
$$= 2\cdot 3 xy^3 - 2x^1 x^2 y^3 + 2\cdot 7 x^1 x^1 y^3 y^5 + 2xy^3 y^1$$
$$= 6xy^3 - 2x^3 y^3 + 14 x^2 y^8 + 2xy^4$$

Try it:

$$4x^2 w^5 (w - x^2 + 6xw^2 - 1 + 3x^4 w^8)$$

Polynomials - Multiplying Easy Ones

Polynomials - Multiplying with FOIL

We've got a cool little trick called "FOIL" for multiplying two binomials

$$(2x+3)(x-5)$$

It's really just an easy way to do the distributive property twice -- which would be really messy and confusing.

Check it out:

$(2x+3)(x-5) = 2x^2$
  └─FIRST─┘   F

$(2x+3)(x-5) = 2x^2 - 10x$
  └───OUTER───┘   F   O

$(2x+3)(x-5) = 2x^2 - 10x + 3x$
     └INNER┘   F   O   I

$(2x+3)(x-5) = 2x^2 - 10x + 3x - 15$
       └LAST┘   F   O   I   L

$ = 2x^2 - 7x - 15$ done!

POLYNOMIALS, FACTORING AND DIVISION

Here's another one:

$$(3x-4)(2x+1)$$

$(3x-4)(2x+1) = 6x^2$
   F

$(3x-4)(2x+1) = 6x^2 + 3x$
   O

$(3x-4)(2x+1) = 6x^2 + 3x - 8x$
   I

$(3x-4)(2x+1) = 6x^2 + 3x - 8x - 4$
   L

$\qquad\qquad\qquad\quad = 6x^2 - 5x - 4$

Try it:

$(5x+3)(2x-7)$

Here's a messier one:

$(2a-5b)(7a+b) = 14a^2 + 2ab - 35ab - 5b^2$
$\qquad\qquad\qquad\quad$ F $\qquad$ O $\qquad$ I

$\qquad\qquad\qquad = 14a^2 - 33ab - 5b^2$

Polynomials - Multiplying with FOIL

Your turn:

$(10w + 3z)(w - 6z)$

FOIL is really just a matching game that matches each guy in the first chunk to each guy in the second chunk:

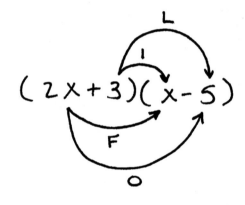

Polynomials - Multiplying Messier Ones

This is similar to FOIL -- it's a matching game. We just have more guys to match. Check it out:

$$(2x+3)(4x^2-x+5)$$

We'll start by matching the $2x$ to each guy in the second chunk:

$$(2x+3)(4x^2-x+5) = 8x^3 - 2x^2 + 10x \ldots$$

Then, we match the 3 to each guy in the second chunk:

$$(2x+3)(4x^2-x+5) = 8x^3 - 2x^2 + 10x$$
$$+ 12x^2 - 3x + 15$$

Now, just add like terms...
$$= 8x^3 + 10x^2 + 7x + 15$$

Try it:

$$(x+3)(4x^2-2x+6)$$

There's another way to do these -- it might help you keep better track of the details.

Remember how to multiply this guy by hand? Do it!

$$\begin{array}{r} 239 \\ \times\ 46 \\ \hline \end{array}$$

Well, we can just stack the polynomials and do it the same way!

Check it out:

$$\begin{array}{r} 4x^2 - 2x + 6 \\ \otimes \quad\quad x + 3 \\ \hline 12x^2 - 6x + 18 \\ +\ 4x^3 - 2x^2 + 6x \quad\quad\quad \\ \hline 4x^3 + 10x^2 + 0 + 18 \end{array}$$

← This let's you stack the like terms.

answer: $4x^3 + 10x^2 + 18$

I call this the "stacking" method.

---

112   POLYNOMIALS, FACTORING AND DIVISION   **112**

Factoring - What's a Factor Again?

From way back in 3rd grade...

$$3 \cdot 2 = 6$$

These are the factors of 6.   This is the product.

It works the same way with messier factors...

$$2w^3 y^4 z$$

factors

$$2x(3y+5) = 6xy + 10x$$

factors

$$(x-3)(x+7) = x^2 + 4x - 21$$

factors

$$(5x-1)(2x+3) = 10x^2 + 13x - 3$$

factors

$$(x-1)(x^2 + x + 1) = x^3 - 1$$

factors

Factoring - Undoing the Distributive Property

Let's just dive right in!

What can you undistribute (no, that's not a real word) in this?

$$2x + 2y$$

$$2x + 2y = 2(x+y)$$

The 2!

If you don't believe me, distribute the 2 back in to see if it works.

This is one of the main games of factoring -- undistributing things. We'll call it "taking out" or "factoring out."

What can we take out of this?

$$5x^2 + 10x$$

$$5x^2 + 10x = 5x(x+2)$$

a $5x$!

OK, now check this guy out -- and be careful! Always distribute to check it.

$$9x^2 - 3x$$

$$9x^2 - 3x = 3x(3x - 1)$$

We need this guy as a placeholder!

Try it:

$$\text{Factor } 2x^2 - 4x$$

$$\text{Factor } 7x + 14x^2$$

The thing to remember on these is that, for something to be factored out, it has to be in <u>every</u> term.

Here's something messier:

What can we factor out of this?

$$2x^2y^5 - 4xy^3 + 6x^4y^2$$

Look at the numbers (coefficients) first:

a 2 comes out

Now, look at the x's:

$$x^2 \qquad x \qquad x^4$$

They all have one x... So, an x comes out.

Finally, the y's:

$$y^5 \qquad y^3 \qquad y^2$$

They all have a y^2...

Factoring - Undoing the Distributive Property

Altogether, we'll factor out a
$$2xy^2$$

$$2x^2y^5 - 4xy^3 + 6x^4y^2 = 2xy^2(\qquad\qquad)$$

↗ Now we just have to figure out what goes in here.

Think backwards -- and always keep distributing in mind.

Look at the first term:

We took $2xy^2$ out of $2x^2y^5$

What would be left?

Or...

What would we need to multiply $2xy^2$ by to get back up to $2x^2y^5$?

We need another x... and a y^3...

$$2x^2y^5 - 4xy^3 + 6x^4y^2 = 2xy^2(\, xy^3 \qquad\quad)$$

↖ ↗ check by distributing.

Now, the second term:

We took $2xy^2$ out of $-4xy^3$

So, we need a -2... and a y...

$$2x^2y^5 - 4xy^3 + 6x^4y^2 = 2xy^2(\, xy^3 - 2y \quad)$$

check it!

And the last term:

We took $2xy^2$ out of $6x^4y^2$

So, we need a 3... and an x^3...

$$2x^2y^5 - 4xy^3 + 6x^4y^2 = 2xy^2(xy^3 - 2y + 3x^3)$$

Check it! Does it work? Yep!

Your turn:

Factor $15a^2b^4 - 5ab^3 + 20a^3b^3 + 10a^5b^7$

Factor $6x^4y^3 + 2x^2y^2 - 8x^5y^6$

* Be careful! You'll need to have three terms in your ( ) since we started with three terms.

Remember this -- it will keep popping up:

> The First Rule of Factoring:
>
> Always see if you can factor something out of all the terms. If you can, don't just sit there with your finger up your nose --
> DO IT!

Factoring - Undoing the Distributive Property

Factoring - Intro to Trinomials

Remember that a trinomial has three terms. Like this guy:

$$x^2 - 3x - 10$$

Right now, we're really interested in a certain type of trinomial...

$$x^2 - 3x - 10$$

a squared guy → x^2
a regular guy → $-3x$
a number guy → -10

Remember FOIL?
We can multiply

$$(x-5)(x+2) \text{ and get } x^2 - 3x - 10$$

Hey -- that's our trinomial from above. Basically, we'll be figuring out how to "undo" guys like

$$x^2 - 3x - 10$$

into their factors: $(x-5)(x+2)$

You'll mostly be needing to know how to do this to solve equations like

$$x^2 - 3x - 10 = 0$$

(which we'll do later)

Here's the deal though -- and I'm going to be honest with you...

Most trinomials guys <u>won't</u> factor!

Oh, they will in your math class because books and teachers design them that way.

But, out in the real world of business and science, they won't.

In your math classes, it will be an OK thing to learn... just because it will save you some time.

Guys with just an x^2 in front, like

$$x^2 - 3x - 10$$

will be pretty easy to factor (or you'll be able to see quickly that they won't factor.)

Guys with a number in front of the x^2, like

$$5x^2 - 13x - 6$$

will be harder.

When you get to solve equations...

$$5x^2 - 13x - 6 = 0$$

I'll tell you to give it a 10 second factor attempt. If you can't pop it, there's a formula that will kill it every time.

Factoring - Intro to Trinomials

Life's too short to spend 20 minutes trying to factor something.

Hey, you could get run over by a bus right after... and you would have wasted the last 20 minutes of your life!

FOR MORE ALGEBRA PRACTICE PROBLEMS, CHECK OUT MY

Algebra Crunchers

Generate an endless number of algebra problems -- with hints and answers, so you can check your work!

Coolmath.com/crunchers

Factoring - Trinomials - Undoing FOIL

Do you really remember FOIL?
Prove it by multiplying these:

$(x-5)(x+2) =$

$(x+3)(x+3) =$

$(x-6)(x-7) =$

$(x+8)(x+1) =$

OK, now we'll be undoing FOIL. I'm going to merge you into this slowly. Factoring can be a bit of a shock.

Remember that, when you do FOIL, there are inner and outer terms... This will be the key to nailing these things.

Let's try to factor this guy:

$$x^2 - 4x - 45$$

I'm going to start you out...
First, we can do the x guys -- they're easy:

$(x\quad)(x\quad)$

And I'm going to give you the last guys:

$(x\ 5)(x\ 9)$

Now, look at the last term of our trinomial: -45

$$x^2 - 4x - 45 \leftarrow \text{last}$$
$$\uparrow$$
middle

and our middle coefficient: -4

All we need to do is figure out what signs to put in this

$$(x \quad 5)(x \quad 9)$$

to give both the -45 and the -4...

It can't be

$$(x+5)(x+9)$$

because this would give us a positive 45.

For the same reason, it can't be

$$(x-5)(x-9)$$

We need to use a $+$ and a $-$...
and we need a -4...

$$+5 - 9 = -4$$
and
$$(+5)(-9) = -45$$

So,

$$x^2 - 4x - 45 = (x+5)(x-9)$$

check it with FOIL!

Let's try another one:

Factor $x^2 + 7x + 12$

I'll give you a big start:
$$(x \quad 3)(x \quad 4)$$
What do you think?

    The 12 is positive...
    and we need a +7...

Will this work?
$$(x+3)(x-4)$$
    No! It gives a last term of −12.

Will this work?
$$(x-3)(x+4)$$
    No! Same reason.

What about this?
$$(x-3)(x-4)$$
    The last term _is_ a positive 12...
    But, the outer and inner terms give −7... So, no!

How about this? (It's our last chance!)
$$(x+3)(x+4)$$
Check it with FOIL... It works!

Factoring − Undoing FOIL

Try it:

  Factor $x^2 - x - 20 = (x \quad 4)(x \quad 5)$

  Factor $a^2 - 5a - 24 = (a \quad 3)(a \quad 8)$

Now, I'll take a crutch away...

  Let's factor $x^2 - 4x - 12$

I'll give you

$$(x \quad 2)(x \quad)$$

↗ We need this guy and the signs.

What goes in here?

$$(2)(\;) = 12$$

$$(x \quad 2)(x \quad 6)$$

What about the signs?

  The last term is -12.

  The middle coefficient is -4.

Since the last term is negative, we need a $+$ and a $-$.

Which is it?

$$(-2)(6) = -12 \quad \text{or} \quad (2)(-6) = -12$$

$-2 + 6 = 4$ ↑ This is it since $2 - 6 = -4$

So $x^2 - 4x - 12 = (x+2)(x-6)$

Your turn:

Factor $y^2 + 8y + 15 = (y \ 3)(y \ \ )$

Factor $x^2 - x - 90 = (x \ \ )(x \ 10)$

Now, let's work from scratch!

Factor $x^2 - 6x + 5$

We start with

$(x \ \ )(x \ \ )$

Our last term is 5... our only choice is

$1 \cdot 5$

The 5 has to be positive...

$(-1)(-5) = 5 \quad \text{or} \quad (1)(5) = 5$

The middle guy is -6.
↘ $-1 - 5 = -6$

So $x^2 - 6x + 5 = (x-1)(x-5)$

That one was pretty easy since 5 is prime.

Try it:

Factor $y^2 + 10y - 11$

Here's a harder one:

Factor $a^2 + 7a + 10$

We start with

$(a\ \ )(a\ \ )$

Our last term is 10... so, our choices are

$1 \cdot 10$ and $2 \cdot 5$

Which is it? Our middle guy will guide us...

We need a 7.

Can we use a 1 and a 10 to make a 7? No! So, it's the 2 and the 5:

$(a\ \ 2)(a\ \ 5)$

What about the signs?

$+2 + 5 = +7$

So, $a^2 + 7a + 10 = (a+2)(a+5)$

Your turn:
$$\text{Factor } x^2 - 20x - 21$$

This one's harder:
$$\text{Factor } b^2 - 7b + 12$$

This one has more possibilities for the 12:

$$1 \cdot 12 \quad \text{and} \quad 2 \cdot 6 \quad \text{and} \quad 3 \cdot 4$$

Which pair will score us a -7 for the middle guy?

$$3 \text{ and } 4$$

$$(-3)(-4) = 12 \quad\quad -3 - 4 = -7$$

$$\text{so } b^2 - 7b + 12 = (b-3)(b-4)$$

Try it:
$$\text{Factor } y^2 + 12y - 28$$

Here's one last weird thing on these:
$$\text{Factor } x^2 - 5xy - 36y^2$$

This is different!

Factoring – Undoing FOIL

Since we have a back variable, we just start with

$$(x \quad y)(x \quad y)$$

Our possibilities for the 36 are

$$1 \cdot 36 \quad 2 \cdot 18 \quad 3 \cdot 12 \quad 4 \cdot 9 \quad 6 \cdot 6$$

Which pair will get us a -5?

4 and 9

$$(4)(-9) = -36 \quad 4 - 9 = -36$$

So $x^2 - 5xy - 36y^2 = (x+4y)(x-9y)$

FOIL this so you'll believe the y thing!

Your turn:

Factor $a^2 - 8ab - 48b^2$

As I said before, except for in math classes, these things don't factor.
So, we have to be prepared to prove this!

Try to factor this guy:
$$x^2 - 4x + 5$$

We start with this:
$$(x\ \ )(x\ \ )$$

Obviously, this is our only option:
$$(x\ \ 1)(x\ \ 5)$$

Hmm... It sure looks like it will factor...
$$(x-5)(x+1) = x^2 - 4x - 5$$

We got the -4!   oops!

Since our possibilities are shot, this thing won't factor.

Factoring - Harder Trinomials

Now, we're going to learn how to factor guys with a number in front of the x^2...

$$5x^2 - 8x + 3$$

I'm not going to lie to you -- these can be pretty tricky. Some students don't like these because there is no way to just memorize how to do them. Each problem is different and you just have to figure it out!

There *is* a basic strategy for successfully conquering these ... It's not great, but, it's really all we have.

Let's just dive in. I'm going to start with prime numbers at first to ease you in.

Let's factor this guy:

$$5x^2 - 8x + 3$$

Remember, that we are undoing FOIL

( )( )

These first guys will have to give us $5x^2$

Since 5 is prime, our only choice is

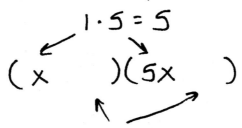

$1 \cdot 5 = 5$

$(x \quad)(5x \quad)$

These last guys will have to give us a 3...

Since 3 is prime, our only choice is

$1 \cdot 3$

But, which guy goes in which spot?

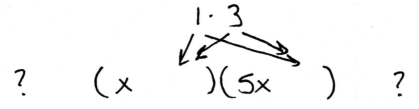

$1 \cdot 3$

? $(x \quad)(5x \quad)$?

Well, let's just see which works!

We need the middle term to be $-8x$.

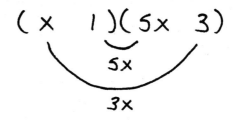

$(x \quad 3)(5x \quad 1)$ $(x \quad 1)(5x \quad 3)$

    15x   5x

      x   3x

We cannot get a $-8x$ using x and $15x$. $-3x - 5x = -8x$

Factoring - Harder Trinomials

So, $5x^2 - 8x + 3 = (x-1)(5x-3)$

* Always double check this last term! Does it give a +3?

Here's another one:

Factor $7x^2 + 76x - 11$

Our only choice for the first guy is

$(x \quad)(7x \quad)$

For the last guy, our only choice is

$1 \cdot 11$

We need a middle guy of $76x$.
Which one of these will work?

$(x \quad 1)(7x \quad 11)$
  $7x$
  $11x$

We cannot get a $76x$ using $7x$ and $11x$.

$(x \quad 11)(7x \quad 1)$
  $77x$
  x

$77x - x = 76x$

↗ the inside is positive

↑ the outside is negative

So $7x^2 + 76x - 11 = (x+11)(7x-1)$
   check it with FOIL!

Your turn:
   Factor $3x^2 - 4x - 7$

   Factor $5x^2 + 36x + 7$

Let's make it a little harder...
   Factor $2x^2 - x - 6$

Our only choice for the first guy is

$$\overset{1 \cdot 2}{(x \quad)(2x \quad)}$$

Since 6 is not prime, we have more choices to worry about:
   $1 \cdot 6$ and $2 \cdot 3$

Factoring - Harder Trinomials

But... which pair and in what order?

Here's the best way to figure it out:

make a list of possibilities... work through it until we hit the right one.

First guys	Possible last guys
1·2	1·6
	6·1
	2·3
	3·2

Notice that I switched these -- to check ALL possible combos.

Now, we just go through each one -- doing FOIL...

We need a middle guy of $-x$... So, -1

①  2 and 6 cannot make a -1.

②  12 and 1 cannot make a -1.

③ 1·2 and 2·3
   with products 4 and 3

$3 - 4 = -1$
We have a winner!

---

134   POLYNOMIALS, FACTORING AND DIVISION   134

Now that we have the numbers, lock them in like this:

$$\underline{\text{First}} \qquad \underline{\text{Last}}$$
$$1 \cdot 2 \qquad 2 \cdot 3$$

$$(x-2)(2x+3)$$

with $-4x$ and $3x$ cross terms.

So, $2x^2 - x - 6 = (x-2)(2x+3)$ ✓ with FOIL!

Try it:

Factor $3x^2 - 2x - 8$

Here's another one:

Factor $4x^2 - 16x + 7$

Since the last guy is prime, let's lock him down first:

$$(\quad 1)(\quad 7)$$

Now, we need to find the first guys...
our choices are:

$$1 \cdot 4 \quad \text{and} \quad 2 \cdot 2$$

Here's our list of possible combinations:

First	Last
1·4	1·7
4·1	
2·2	

We need a middle guy of −16...

① 1·4 and 1·7   4 and 7 cannot
       4   make a −16.
       7

② 4·1 and 1·7   1 and 28 cannot
       1   make a −16
       28

③ 2·2 and 1·7   −2 −14 = −16
       2
       14

See if you can lock them in... I'll do it on the next page.

Lock them in:

$$\underset{\downarrow}{\overset{\overset{\text{First}}{2\cdot 2}}{}}\ \underset{\downarrow}{\overset{\overset{\text{Last}}{1\cdot 7}}{}}$$

$(2x-1)(2x-7)$

with cross-multiplication giving $-2x$ and $-14x$

So, $4x^2 - 16x + 7 = (2x-1)(2x-7)$

Try it:

Factor $12x^2 - 17x - 5$

OK... Now let's leave the safe world of primes behind! Ready? Do you need an antacid or anything? If you start to hyperventilate at anytime, breathe into a paper bag.

Let's factor this guy:

$$4x^2 + 11x + 6$$

Factoring - Harder Trinomials

Possible First guys	Possible Last guys
1·4	1·6
2·2	2·3

Since we'll need to check all possible combos, we need to flip one set of these. For this one, the first guys are easier:

First	Last
1·4	1·6
4·1	2·3
2·2	

Now, we just need to start running through the list until something hits.

Our middle guy is 11x.

Here's how I run through them:

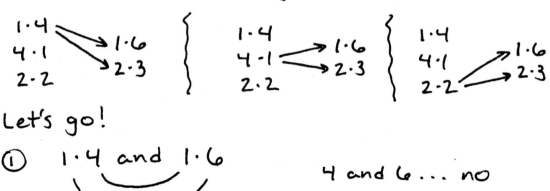

Let's go!

① 1·4 and 1·6   4 and 6 ... no
      4
      6

② 1·4 and 2·3   8 + 3 = 11
   (8, 3 shown under arcs)   That popped fast!

Lock them in:

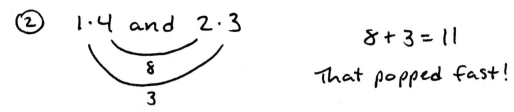

First   Last
1·4   2·3
  ↓ ✕ ↓
(x + 2)(4x + 3)
       8x
      3x

So, $4x^2 + 11x + 6 = (x+2)(4x+3)$
                      ✓ with FOIL!

Let's try another one:

Factor $8w^2 - 6w - 9$

Possible   Possible
First guys   Last guys

1·8   1·9
2·4   3·3
                  ↗
            Easiest to flip these.

First	Last
1·8	1·9
2·4	9·1
	3·3

Our middle guy is $-6w$

① 1·8 and 1·9 → 8 and 9 ... no
② 1·8 and 9·1 → 72 and 1 ... no
③ 1·8 and 3·3 → 24 and 3 ... no
④ 2·4 and 1·9 → 4 and 18 ... no
⑤ 2·4 and 9·1 → 36 and 2 ... no
⑥ 2·4 and 3·3 → 12 and 6 ...

$$\boxed{-12 + 6 = -6}$$

First	Last
2·4	3·3

$$(2w-3)(4w+3)$$

$-12w$
$6w$

So, $8w^2 - 6w - 9 = (2w-3)(4w+3)$

POLYNOMIALS, FACTORING AND DIVISION

Your turn:

Factor $6x^2 + 11x - 10$

* make your list and work through it -- don't just guess and hope for the best!

Sometimes (even in math books) these things don't factor. So... when you are taking a test and you can't figure out if something will factor or not, what will you do?

- (a) cry
- (b) mumble words that would shock your grandma
- (c) work through your list and know, for sure, that it really won't factor

I'd go with choice (c) if I were you.

Factoring - Harder Trinomials

Check this out:

Factor $15x^2 + 7x + 4$

First	Last
1·15	1·4
3·5	4·1
	2·2

We need a 7x.

① 1·15 and 1·4 → 15 and 4... no
② 1·15 and 4·1 → 60 and 1... no
③ 1·15 and 2·2 → 30 and 2... no
④ 3·5 and 1·4 → 5 and 12...

$-5 + 12 = 7$

First   Last
3·5   1·4

$(3x - 1)(5x + 4)$

$-5x$
$12x$

✓ with FOIL: $(3x-1)(5x+4)$
$= 15x^2 + 7x - 4$ ← NO!

Dead end -- keep going!

⑤ 3·5 and 4·1 → 20 and 3... no
⑥ 3·5 and 2·2 → 10 and 6... NO!

That's it! All possibilities have been exhausted. No sweating on the test -- I'm sure!

This thang doesn't factor, Baby!

Your turn:

Prove that $7x^2 - 33x + 10$ does <u>not</u> factor.

Factoring - Special Guys

Before I show you any special guys, you need to be very familiar with some basic perfect squares:

$1^2 = 1$	$2^2 = 4$	$3^2 = 9$	$4^2 = 16$
$5^2 = 25$	$6^2 = 36$	$7^2 = 49$	$8^2 = 64$
$9^2 = 81$	$10^2 = 100$	$11^2 = 121$	$12^2 = 144$

And some perfect cubes:

$1^3 = 1$	$2^3 = 8$	$3^3 = 27$
$4^3 = 64$	$5^3 = 125$	

You should know these cold. If my cat comes into your room some night, wakes you out of a dead sleep and yells, "meow meow meow meow!" OK, pretend that he speaks english and yells, "64! What is it? WHAT IS IT?!" Without even thinking, you should yell, "A perfect square! Don't hurt me!"

(Don't worry. My cat isn't allowed out at night.)

OK -- let's go.

Special Guy #1:

> The difference of two squares
> $$x^2 - a^2 = (x-a)(x+a)$$

Check it out:

Factor $x^2 - 9$

Write it as $x^2 - 3^2$... (a ↗)

$$x^2 - 9 = x^2 - 3^2 = (x-3)(x+3)$$

✓ using FOIL -- Believe me?

Try it:

Factor $y^2 - 16$

Here's another one:

Factor $25b^2 - 1$

Rewrite it as squares...

$$25b^2 - 1 = (5b)^2 - 1^2 = (5b-1)(5b+1)$$

↘ $5 \cdot 5 \cdot b \cdot b$ ↗

Your turn:

Factor $4x^2 - 81$

Factoring - Special Guys

What about this guy?

$$x^2 + 4$$
↑ plus!

What did we call special guy #1?

The <u>difference</u> of two squares!

x^2+4 is a sum -- not a difference... and we do <u>not</u> know how to factor him yet!
(Later!)

Special Guy #2:

$$\boxed{\text{The difference of two cubes} \\ x^3 - a^3 = (x-a)(x^2 + ax + a^2)}$$

↗ memorize this puppy or you're dead meat on the test!

Check it out:

$$\text{Factor } x^3 - 8$$

Rewrite it as cubes...

$$x^3 - 8 = x^3 - 2^3 = (x-2)(x^2 + 2x + (2)^2)$$
$$= (x-2)(x^2 + 2x + 4)$$

* multiply it back out to check!

Here's another one:

$$\text{Factor } 27y^3 - 64$$

Rewrite it as cubes:

$$27y^3 - 64 = (3y)^3 - 4^3$$
$$= (3y-4)((3y)^2 + (4)(3y) + (4)^2)$$
$$= (3y-4)(9y^2 + 12y + 16)$$

↗ By the way, this trinomial part will never factor. NEVER!

Try it:

$$\text{Factor } 125x^3 - 1$$

Special Guy #3:

$$\boxed{\begin{array}{c} \text{The sum of two cubes} \\ x^3 + a^3 = (x+a)(x^2 - ax + a^2) \end{array}}$$

↗ Know it. Love it.

Check it out:

$$\text{Factor } 8w^3 + 1$$

Rewrite it as cubes...

$$8w^3 + 1 = (2w)^3 + 1$$
$$= (2w+1)((2w)^2 - (1)(2w) + 1^2)$$
$$= (2w+1)(4w^2 - 2w + 1)$$

✓ it by multiplying!

Here's another one:

Factor $27x^3 + 64y^3$

Rewrite it as cubes...

$$27x^3 + 64y^3 = (3x)^3 + (4y)^3$$
$$= (3x+4y)((3x)^2 - (4y)(3x) + (4y)^2)$$
$$= (3x+4y)(9x^2 - 12xy + 16y^2)$$

Your turn:

Factor $8a^3 + b^3$

There is one thing I need to tell you:

The <u>only</u> place you'll ever see these cubed special guys is in math books!

Factoring - By Grouping

Something like this will pop up on you if you go on to take Calculus... Other than that, you probably won't see it anywhere.

Let's start out very simply...

Factor these:

$$5w + 3xw = \underline{\hspace{3cm}}$$

$$5y^2 + 3xy^2 = \underline{\hspace{3cm}}$$

$$5k^3 + 3xk^3 = \underline{\hspace{3cm}}$$

Now, can you do these?

$$5(\text{blob}) + 3x(\text{blob}) = \underline{\hspace{3cm}}$$

$$5(w+2) + 3x(w+2) = \underline{\hspace{3cm}}$$

This type of guy will show up half way through this process... You just did the last step of factoring by grouping. Aren't you thrilled?

Here are some more last-step guys:

$$2w(x+5) + 7(x+5) = (x+5)(2w+7)$$

factor the (x+5) blob out.

$$x^2(y-3) - 8(y-3) = (y-3)(x^2-8)$$

factor the (y-3) blob out.

Try it:

Factor $3x^3(x-6) + 4(x-6)$

Factor $9y(w^2+1) - 4x(w^2+1)$

Now that we have that part down, let's start from the beginning.
These guys always have four terms...
Like this guy:

$$5w + 10 + 3xw + 6x$$

Here's the plan of attack:

$$5w + 10 + 3xw + 6x$$

Can you factor something out of these two terms? DO IT!

Can you factor something out of these two terms? DO IT!

$$= 5(w+2) + 3x(w+2)$$

Look familiar?
Now, just factor the blob out:

$$= (w+2)(5+3x)$$

*multiply it all out to check!

Let's do another one:

Factor $2wx + 10w + 7x + 35$

$\underbrace{2wx + 10w}_{\text{factor}} + \underbrace{7x + 35}_{\text{factor}} = 2w(x+5) + 7(x+5)$

$= (x+5)(2w+7)$ done!

Not bad, is it?

Here's one more:

Factor $x^2y - 3x^2 - 8y + 24$

$\underbrace{x^2y - 3x^2} \underbrace{- 8y + 24} = x^2(y-3)$

There's one thing to watch out for here...
The back blobs <u>have</u> to match!
So, what needs to come out of the second set?

$= x^2(y-3) - 8(y-3)$

Does this sign work? Distribute to check.

$= (y-3)(x^2-8)$

Your turn:

Factor $3x^4 - 18x^3 + 4x - 24$

Factoring - By Grouping

Factor $9yw^2 + 9y - 4xw^2 - 4x$

Factoring - A Final Overview

Now that you've learned each factoring technique, the trick is to know which one to use and when!

Let's run down the list:

Rule #1:

> The first rule of factoring: Always see if you can factor something out of <u>all</u> the terms.

example: $6x^2y + 9x^3y^4 - 3xy$
$= 3xy(2x + 3x^2y^3 - 1)$

This often occurs along with another type of factoring.

example: $2x^3 - 2x^2 - 12x$
$= 2x(x^2 - x - 6) = 2x(x-3)(x+2)$

* All of the rest of the rules assume that you've done Rule #1 first.

Rule #2:

> If it has two terms, it's probably one of the special guys.

example: $9a^2 - 1$

$= (3a)^2 - 1 = (3a-1)(3a+1)$

example: $2x^4 - 16x$

$= 2x(x^3 - 8) = 2x(x^3 - 2^3)$
$= 2x(x-2)(x^2 + 2x + 4)$

example: $27w^3 + 1$

$= (3w)^3 + 1 = (3w+1)(9w^2 - 3w + 1)$

RULE #3:

> If it has three terms and the coefficient on the squared guy is 1...
> Then, it's a NIKE factor.
> JUST DO IT!

example: $y^2 + 8y + 7$

$= (y+1)(y+7)$

RULE #4:

> If it has three terms and the coefficient on the squared guy is not a 1...
> Make your list and start hammering!

POLYNOMIALS, FACTORING AND DIVISION

example: $6x^2 - 19x - 7$

First	Last
1·6	1·7
2·3	7·1

We need a -19...

① 1·6 and 1·7 → 6 and 7... no
② 1·6 and 7·1 → 42 and 1... no
③ 2·3 and 1·7 → 3 and 14... no
④ 2·3 and 7·1 → 21 and 2...

$-21 + 2 = -19$

First: 2·3   Last: 7·1

$(2x - 7)(3x + 1)$

$-21x$
$2x$

So, $6x^2 - 19x - 7 = (2x - 7)(3x + 1)$

example: $3x^2 - 9x - 12$ *RULE 1!*

$= 3(x^2 - 3x - 4) = 3(x+1)(x-4)$

Now, it's just a NIKE factor.

---

155   Factoring — A Final Overview   155

RULE #5:

> If it's got four terms, it's probably a factor by grouping guy.

example: $3xy + 15y + 2x + 10$

$= 3y(x+5) + 2(x+5) = (x+5)(3y+2)$

FOR MORE ALGEBRA PRACTICE PROBLEMS, CHECK OUT MY

Algebra Crunchers

Generate an endless number of algebra problems -- with hints and answers, so you can check your work!

Coolmath.com/crunchers

Division – Dividing by Monomials

Remember that monomials are single term critters:

$$x^2 - 3x + 7 \leftarrow \underline{\text{tri}}\text{nomial}$$

$$x + 5 \leftarrow \underline{\text{bi}}\text{nomial}$$

$$6x^2 \leftarrow \underline{\text{mono}}\text{mial}$$

Dividing by these things pops up fairly often in later math classes.

Let's just do one:

$$(18x^4 - 10x^2 + 6x^7) \div 2x^2$$

Let's rewrite it like this:

$$\frac{18x^4 - 10x^2 + 6x^7}{2x^2}$$

Since there is only one term down here, we can break this thing up...

$$\frac{18x^4 - 10x^2 + 6x^7}{2x^2} = \frac{18x^4}{2x^2} - \frac{10x^2}{2x^2} + \frac{6x^7}{2x^2}$$

Now, we just reduce each term!

$$= 9x^2 - 5 + 3x^5$$

It's that simple!

Here's another one:

$$(5xy^2 - 12x^3y^4 - 6) \div 3x$$

$$\frac{5xy^2 - 12x^3y^4 - 6}{3x} = \frac{5xy^2}{3x} - \frac{12x^3y^4}{3x} - \frac{6}{3x}$$

$$= \frac{5}{3}y^2 - 4x^2y^4 - \frac{2}{x}$$

Try it:

$$(4wy^2 - 20w^2 + 6wy - 7) \div 4wy^2$$

By the way, if you don't believe that we can really break these things up... Just try it with some regular numbers:

$$\frac{1+3}{2} = \frac{1}{2} + \frac{3}{2} = 2$$

Heck, we do this with fractions all the time!

Division - Long Division

Remember how to do long division?
Do this guy to get your brain going again:

$$3\overline{)78921}$$

Long division with polynomials works the same way. You just have to deal with x junk along the way.

Let's walk through one:

$$(2x^2 + 7x - 15) \div (x+5)$$

Set it up:

$$x+5\overline{)2x^2+7x-15}$$

The first thing we do is see how many times this guy goes into this guy

So, we are looking at $2x^2 \div x$ ...

The easiest thing to do is to write it like

$$\frac{2x^2}{x}$$ and reduce... $2x$ ← put it here

$$x+5 \overline{\smash{)}2x^2+7x-15}^{\,2x}$$

Now, do what you did with regular long division:

multiply these → $2x$

$$x+5 \overline{\smash{)}2x^2+7x-15}$$

→ Then, stick the product here and subtract.

$$\begin{array}{r} 2x \\ x+5 \overline{\smash{)}2x^2+7x-15} \\ -(2x^2+10x) \\ \hline -3x \end{array}$$

↗ These should subtract out.

Before we go on, I want to point out something very important to you...

$$\begin{array}{r} 2x \\ x+5 \overline{\smash{)}2x^2+7x-15} \\ -(2x^2+10x) \end{array}$$

→ See these parenthesis? If you don't put them in, you'll do the entire problem WRONG! Why?

Division - Long Division

Because that minus distributes into the second guy!

$$-(2x^2 + 10x)$$

So, raise your right hand. Come on! Do it! Repeat after me:

> "I promise to always put my parenthesis in... Otherwise, I'm just a big goof!"

Back to the problem: (where were we?) Oh yeah!

$$\begin{array}{r} 2x \\ x+5 \overline{\smash{)}\,2x^2+7x-15} \\ -(2x^2+10x) \\ \hline -3x \end{array}$$

Now, we see how many times this guy goes into this guy.

$$\frac{-3x}{x} = -3$$

$$\begin{array}{r} 2x - 3 \\ x+5 \overline{\smash{)}\,2x^2+7x-15} \end{array}$$

$$x+5 \overline{\smash{\big)}\, 2x^2+7x-15}^{\;2x-3}$$
$$\underline{-(2x^2+10x)} \downarrow \text{ Bring this down.}$$
$$ -3x-15$$

~~~~~~~~~~~~~~~~~~~~~~~~~~~~~

$\overset{\text{multiply}}{\curvearrowright}$

$$x+5 \overline{\smash{\big)}\, 2x^2+7x-15}^{\;2x-3}$$
$$\underline{-(2x^2+10x)}$$
$$ -3x-15$$
and subtract → $ \underline{-(-3x-15)}$
$$ \rightarrow 0$$

When you hit 0, and there are no guys left to bring down, you're done!

So, $(2x^2+7x-15) \div (x+5) = 2x-3$

Check it by multiplying!

$$(2x-3)(x+5) = 2x^2+10x-3x-15$$
$$= 2x^2+7x-15 \text{ yep!}$$

Here's another one:

$$\frac{14x^4-5x^3-11x^2-11x+8}{2x-1}$$

Division - Long Division

set it up:

$$2x-1 \overline{\smash{\big)}\, 14x^4 - 5x^3 - 11x^2 - 11x + 8}$$

↗ ↗
This into this

$$\boxed{\dfrac{14x^4}{2x} = 7x^3}$$

---

① multiply
$$\begin{array}{r} 7x^3 \\ 2x-1 \overline{\smash{\big)}\, 14x^4 - 5x^3 - 11x^2 - 11x + 8} \\ -(14x^4 - 7x^3) \\ \hline 2x^3 - 11x^2 \end{array}$$

② subtract ③ bring him down

④ this into this ↗

$$\boxed{\dfrac{2x^3}{2x} = x^2}$$

---

① multiply
$$\begin{array}{r} 7x^3 + x^2 \\ 2x-1 \overline{\smash{\big)}\, 14x^4 - 5x^3 - 11x^2 - 11x + 8} \\ -(14x^4 - 7x^3) \\ \hline 2x^3 - 11x^2 \\ -(2x^3 - x^2) \\ \hline -10x^2 - 11x \end{array}$$

② subtract   ③

④ this into this ↗

$$\boxed{\dfrac{-10x^2}{2x} = -5x}$$

POLYNOMIALS, FACTORING AND DIVISION

I'm just going to finish it off:

$$\begin{array}{r}
7x^3 + x^2 - 5x - 8 \\
2x-1 \overline{\smash{)}14x^4 - 5x^3 - 11x^2 - 11x + 8} \\
\underline{-(14x^4 - 7x^3)} \\
2x^3 - 11x^2 \\
\underline{-(2x^3 - x^2)} \\
-10x^2 - 11x \\
\underline{-(-10x^2 + 5x)} \\
-16x + 8 \\
\underline{-(-16x+8)} \\
0
\end{array}$$

So, $\dfrac{14x^4 - 5x^3 - 11x^2 - 11x + 8}{2x-1} = 7x^3 + x^2 - 5x - 8$

check it by multiplying (I'll wait):

$(2x-1)(7x^3 + x^2 - 5x - 8)$

Division - Long Division

Your turn:
$$(15x^3 - 2x^2 + 10x + 12) \div (3x + 2)$$

---

* If you think this is it on these, hold on there, Skippy! You've got two more sections to read.

Division - Long Division - Freaky Things That Can Happen Part 1

Here's one freaky thing that can happen -- and it happens a lot:

Look at this guy...

$$(x^3-8) \div (x-2) \text{ which is } x-2 \overline{\smash{\big)}x^3-8}$$

Whenever you set these guys up, you need two things:

① All the powers in descending order:

$$x^5 \quad x^4 \quad x^3 \quad x^2 \quad x \quad \#$$

② All the powers represented:

For x^3-8, we have no x^2 guy and no x guy...

So, we need to write it as

$$x^3 + 0x^2 + 0x - 8$$

We haven't changed his value... But, we've added some important place-holders. I call them "dummy guys."

If you don't have the dummy guys in the set up, you're going to get stuck with a situation that you don't know how to deal with...

Check it out:

Do the first chunk of the problem with the dummy guys:

$$\begin{array}{r} x^2 \\ x-2 \overline{\smash{\big)}\, x^3+0x^2+0x-8} \\ -(x^3-2x^2) \\ \hline 2x^2 \end{array}$$

← You need an x^2 guy to stick the $-2x^2$ under!

If you didn't have the dummy guy:

$$\begin{array}{r} x^2 \\ x-2 \overline{\smash{\big)}\, x^3-8} \\ -(x^3-2x^2) \\ \hline \uparrow \end{array}$$

No like terms... Very confusing!

Try working the rest of the problem the right way. I'll do it on the next page.

POLYNOMIALS, FACTORING AND DIVISION

$$\begin{array}{r} x^2+2x+4 \\ x-2 \overline{\smash{)}\,x^3+0x^2+0x-8} \\ -(x^3-2x^2) \\ \hline 2x^2+0x \\ -(2x^2-4x) \\ \hline 4x-8 \\ -(4x-8) \\ \hline 0 \end{array}$$

So, $(x^3-8) \div (x-2) = x^2+2x+4$

Your turn:

$$(8x^3-1) \div (2x-1)$$

---

169 — Division – Long Division – Freaky Things That Can Happen Part 1

Division - Long Division - Freaky Things That Can Happen Part 2

So far, when we've been doing these long division things, we've gotten a nice 0 at the end:

$$\overline{} \\ 0$$

This means that the divisor polynomial went into the other guy cleanly -- no remainder.

As you can imagine, things only work out nicely like this when math teachers design them this way! So, we're going to need to learn to deal with remainders.

Let's do a really basic review:

$$15 \div 3 = 5 \leftarrow \text{no remainder}$$

$$15 \div 7 = 2 \text{ with a remainder of } 1$$

For the second one, we're really doing this:

$$\begin{array}{r} 2 \\ 7\overline{)15} \\ -14 \\ \hline 1 \end{array} \leftarrow \text{remainder}$$

We officially write it like this:

$$15 \div 7 = 2\tfrac{1}{7} \quad \begin{array}{l}\leftarrow \text{remainder} \\ \leftarrow \text{original divisor}\end{array}$$

Remember? Well, it works the same way with polynomials.

Let's try one:
$$(x^2 - 9) \div (x + 7)$$

Set it up and remember the dummy guy:

$$x + 7 \overline{\smash{\big)}\, x^2 + 0x - 9}$$

Start working it...

$$\begin{array}{r} x \\ x+7 \overline{\smash{\big)}\, x^2 + 0x - 9} \\ \underline{-(x^2 + 7x)} \\ -7x \end{array}$$

~~~~~~~~~~~~~~~~~~~~~~~~~~~~~~~~~~~~~~

$$\begin{array}{r} x - 7 \\ x+7 \overline{\smash{\big)}\, x^2 + 0x - 9} \\ \underline{-(x^2 + 7x)} \\ -7x - 9 \\ \underline{-(-7x - 49)} \\ 40 \end{array}$$

This does *not* go into this ↑

$\frac{40}{x}$ does *not* reduce!

So, we stop here and the 40 is our remainder. Here's the official answer:

$$(x^2-9) \div (x+7) = x-7+ \frac{40}{x+7}$$

original divisor

Try it:
$$(x^3-2x^2+x-6) \div (x-3)$$

Freaked out by FRACTIONS?

Then get a quick review at
Coolmath.com/fractions

FOR MORE ALGEBRA PRACTICE PROBLEMS,
CHECK OUT MY

Algebra Crunchers

Generate an endless number of algebra problems --
with hints and answers, so you can check your work!

Coolmath.com/crunchers

SOLVING EQUATIONS -AND- INEQUALITIES

Solving Equations - Keep It Balanced

Let's say you've got a see-saw (teeter-totter)... and you've got 50 pounds of stuff piled on each side:

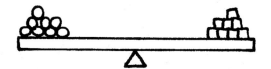

Here's the big algebra game:

> Whatever you do, you've got to keep the see-saw balanced!

What if we add 3 pounds to the left side?

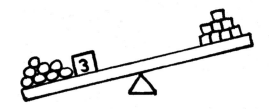

It's not balanced anymore!

But, if we add 3 pounds to both sides?

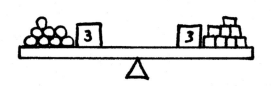

It stays balanced!

Equations are just like see-saws...

You have to keep them balanced!

So, whatever you do to one side of the "=", you've got to do to the other side!

You'll see what it's all about in the next few sections.

Solving Equations - What To Do - Part 1

Let's start with an easy one:

$$\text{Solve } x - 3 = 7$$

We can just look at it and see that $x = 10$...
But, what if we didn't see that? What would we do?

Here's the algebra trick:

We'll add 3 to both sides!

$$\begin{aligned} x - 3 &= 7 \\ +3 & +3 \\ \hline x &= 10 \end{aligned}$$

* Remember the see-saw? Whatever we do to one side, we have to do to the other.

Why did we <u>add</u> 3?

$$x - 3 = 7$$

To undo this!
$+$ is the opposite of $-$

The goal is to get the x alone! Just imagine that Mr. x hasn't showered in a few weeks and everyone wants to get away from him. It's your job to help.

What about this one?
$$x + 5 = 7$$

(Yes, I know you can see that the answer is 2, but, we're learning to play a game here... They're going to get a lot harder.)

Your mission: Get the smelly x alone.

$$x + 5 = 7$$

Who needs to get away? — the +5!

What will undo a +5? a -5!

Do it!

$$\begin{array}{r} x + 5 = 7 \\ -5 \quad -5 \\ \hline x = 2 \end{array}$$ Both sides!

Try it:

Solve $x - 8 = 1$ *show the work!

Here's the first thing we can do:

> We can add or subtract something from both sides!

SOLVING EQUATIONS AND INEQUALITIES

Solving Equations - What To Do - Part 2

We've already learned that we can add or subtract something from both sides of an equation.

So, what if we need to solve something like this?

$$4x = 20$$

(Yep, the answer is 5. I know you can see it... But, we need to learn the game.)

We need to get the x alone...

$$4x = 20$$

We need to get this 4 out of here...
What's he doing to the x? Multiplying!
What's the opposite of multiplying? Dividing!

So, divide both sides by 4:

$$\frac{4x}{4} = \frac{20}{4}$$

Here's what's going on with this thing:

$$\frac{4x}{4} = \frac{4}{4}x = 1x = x$$

$$\text{So } x = 5$$

Here's one that's not so obvious:

Solve $3x = 7$

(Harder to guess the answer now, huh?)

Get the x alone... who's bugging him? the 3

Since the 3 is multiplied with the x... we'll undo him by dividing both sides by 3:

$$\frac{3x}{3} = \frac{7}{3}$$

So $x = \frac{7}{3}$

Hey -- Did you know that you can check these things?

We started with $3x = 7$

and got $x = \frac{7}{3}$ * put it back in!

$3x = 7$

$3(\frac{7}{3}) = 7$

$7 = 7$ Yep - it works!

Try it:

Solve $5x = 13$ * and check it!

Here's another one:

$$\tfrac{1}{4}x = 9$$

There are a couple different ways to deal with this one:

WAY 1:

Rewrite it like this:

$$\tfrac{x}{4} = 9$$

Since the 4 is dividing into the x, we'll multiply both sides by 4 to undo him:

$$4 \cdot \tfrac{x}{4} = 9 \cdot 4$$

$$\tfrac{4}{4} x = 9 \cdot 4$$

$$x = 36$$

WAY 2:

Use the fraction fact that 4 is the multiplicative inverse (big word time!) of $\tfrac{1}{4}$:

$$4 \cdot \tfrac{1}{4} x = 9 \cdot 4$$

$$x = 36$$

$$\boxed{4 \cdot \tfrac{1}{4} = \tfrac{4}{1} \cdot \tfrac{1}{4} = \tfrac{4}{4}}$$

Solving Equations – What To Do – Part 2

Does x = 36 work? Check it!

$$\frac{1}{4}x = 9$$

$$\frac{1}{4}(36) = 9$$

$$\frac{36}{4} = 9 \quad \text{Yep - that's true!}$$

Here's the way you do <u>not</u> want to do this guy!
(And do <u>not</u> let me catch you doing it!)

$$\frac{1}{4}x = 9$$

Do <u>not</u> divide both sides by $\frac{1}{4}$!

$$\frac{\frac{1}{4}x}{\frac{1}{4}} = \frac{9}{\frac{1}{4}} \quad \leftarrow \text{Because, you'll probably mess this thing up...}$$

Especially, if I take your calculator away!

Try it (the right way!)

Solve $\frac{1}{3}x = 8$ *and check it!*

This one's a little harder:

$$\text{Solve } \frac{2}{5}x = 4$$

There are two ways to attack this guy:

WAY 1:

Do it a little at a time...
First, undo the 5:

$$5 \cdot \frac{2}{5}x = 4 \cdot 5$$

$$2x = 20$$

Now, undo the 2:

$$\frac{2x}{2} = 20$$

$$x = 10$$

WAY 2:

Use your knowledge of fractions... and multiplicative inverses:

$$\frac{5}{2} \cdot \frac{2}{5}x = 4 \cdot \frac{5}{2}$$

$$\frac{10}{10}x = \frac{4}{1} \cdot \frac{5}{2}$$

$$x = \frac{20}{2}$$

$$x = 10$$

Your turn:

Solve $\frac{7}{3}x = 14$

WAY 1:

WAY 2:

Here's the second thing we can do:

> We can multiply or divide both sides of an equation by a number.

FOR MORE ALGEBRA PRACTICE PROBLEMS, CHECK OUT MY

Algebra Crunchers

Generate an endless number of algebra problems -- with hints and answers, so you can check your work!

Coolmath.com/crunchers

Solving Equations - What To Do - Putting Parts 1 & 2 Together

Here's our ammunition:

① We can add or subtract a number from both sides of an equation.

② We can multiply or divide both sides of an equation by a number.

* And you always do them in this order!

Now, we'll need to do both.

Check it out:

$$\text{Solve} \quad 2x - 7 = 3$$

Remember our goal: Get the x by himself! There are two guys bugging the x... -7 and 2. The 2 is really locked on and the -7 is, kind of, hanging off... So, we'll go after him first:

$$2x - 7 = 3$$
$$\underline{+7 \quad +7}$$
$$2x = 10$$

Now, ditch the 2:

$$\frac{2x}{2} = \frac{10}{2}$$
$$x = 5$$

check it!
$$2x-7=3 \ldots 2(5)-7=3 \ldots 3=3$$
$$\text{Yep!}$$

Your turn:
$$\text{Solve} \quad 3x+8=-7$$

Here's one with a bit of a twist:
$$\text{Solve} \quad 6-x=7$$

Ditch the 6:
$$6-x=7$$
$$\underline{-6 \quad\quad -6}$$

x isn't quite alone yet!
$$\rightarrow -x=1$$

multiply both sides by -1...
$$(-1)(-x)=(1)(-1)$$
$$x=-1$$

OK, so what if there are x's on both sides?
$$9-3x=5x+6$$

Here's the game: Get all x guys on one side and all number guys on the other.

   ★ Ditch the smallest x guy first! (Trust me.)

Check it out:

$$9 - 3x = 5x + 6$$
$$+3x \quad +3x$$
$$\overline{}$$
$$9 = 8x + 6$$
$$-6 \qquad -6 \qquad \text{ditch the 6}$$
$$\overline{}$$
$$3 = 8x$$
$$\frac{3}{8} = \frac{8x}{8} \qquad \text{ditch the 8}$$
$$\frac{3}{8} = x$$

Check it by sticking it back into both sides:

$$9 - 3x = 5x + 6$$
$$9 - 3\left(\tfrac{3}{8}\right) = 5\left(\tfrac{3}{8}\right) + 6$$
$$9 - \tfrac{9}{8} = \tfrac{15}{8} + 6$$
$$\tfrac{72}{8} - \tfrac{9}{8} = \tfrac{15}{8} + \tfrac{48}{6}$$
$$\tfrac{63}{8} = \tfrac{63}{8} \quad \text{Yep!}$$

Your turn:

Solve $2x + 9 = 6x - 3$

Solving Equations - What To Do - Putting Parts 1 & 2 Together

Solving Equations - Messier Ones

The game is the same... The problems just start out messier.

Let's try one:

Solve $3(2x+5) = 4x+7-x+1$

Start by cleaning up both sides...

$3(2x+5) = 4x+7-x+1$

distribute   add like terms

$$6x+15 = 3x+8$$
$$\underline{-3x \quad\quad -3x\quad\quad}$$ ditch the smallest x

$$3x+15 = 8$$
$$\underline{-15 \quad -15}$$ ditch the 15

$$3x = -7$$

$$\frac{3x}{3} = \frac{-7}{3}$$ ditch the 3

$$x = \frac{-7}{3}$$

I'll let you check it:

Here's another one:

Solve $5x - 3 + 6x + 1 = 5 - 2(x + 4)$

Clean up both sides:

$$11x - 2 = 5 - 2x - 8$$
$$11x - 2 = -2x - 3$$
$$\underline{+2x \qquad\quad +2x}$$ ditch the smallest x
$$13x - 2 = -3$$
$$\underline{+2 \quad +2}$$ ditch the -2
$$13x = -1$$

ditch the 13
$$\frac{13x}{13} = \frac{-1}{13}$$
$$x = \frac{-1}{13}$$

Try it:

Solve $3 - (2x + 5) = 5 + x + 2(4x - 6)$

Solving Equations - Dealing with Fractions & Decimals

Let's start with fractions:

Solve $\dfrac{2}{7} + 3x = 5$

This thing would be a lot easier to solve without this fraction... So, let's make it happen!

If we multiply both sides by 7, we'll be able to ditch that fraction!

Check it out:

$$7\left(\dfrac{2}{7} + 3x\right) = 7(5)$$

$$\dfrac{7 \cdot 2}{7} + 7 \cdot 3x = 7(5)$$

Now, it's like before!

$$2 + 21x = 35$$
$$-2 -2 \quad \text{ditch the 2}$$
$$21x = 33$$

$$\dfrac{21x}{21} = \dfrac{33}{21} \quad \text{ditch the 21}$$

$$x = \dfrac{33}{21} = \dfrac{11}{7}$$

I'll let you check it:

Your turn:
   Solve $5 - \frac{4}{3}x = 2$

Sometimes, there are two fractions to deal with:

   Solve $\frac{3}{5}x + 2 = \frac{1}{4}$

We need to ditch the 5 <u>and</u> the 4...
So, we'll multiply both sides by $5 \cdot 4 = 20$:

$$20\left(\frac{3}{5}x + 2\right) = 20\left(\frac{1}{4}\right)$$

$$\frac{20 \cdot 3}{5}x + 20 \cdot 2 = \frac{20}{4}$$

$$12x + 40 = 5$$

$$\underline{-40 \quad -40} \qquad \text{ditch the 40}$$

$$12x = -35$$

$$\frac{12x}{12} = \frac{-35}{12} \qquad \text{ditch the 12}$$

$$x = \frac{-35}{12}$$

Try it:

Solve $6 - \frac{1}{2}x = \frac{3}{5}$

The next one isn't really that bad, but, it's got a really common mistake spot in it.

Before we start, multiply these numbers for me:

$2 \cdot 3 \cdot 4 = \underline{}$

I hope you got 24!

$2 \cdot 3 \cdot 4 = 6 \cdot 4 = 24$

Never in a million years would you have done it this way:

$2 \cdot 3 \cdot 4 = 2 \cdot 3 \cdot 2 \cdot 4 = 6 \cdot 8 = 48$

≠

It's just plain wrong -- isn't it?

So, don't make this mistake in this next problem!

Solve $\quad \frac{1}{5}x + \frac{1}{3} = \frac{2}{5}(x+4)$

We need to ditch the 3 and the 5...
So, multiply both sides by $3 \cdot 5 = 15$...

$$15\left(\frac{1}{5}x + \frac{1}{3}\right) = 15\left(\frac{2}{5}\right)(x+4)$$

Here's where I don't want you to make the mistake! Think about it!

$$\frac{15}{5}x + \frac{15}{3} = \frac{15 \cdot 2}{5}(x+4)$$

No, you do **not** multiply the 15 into this!

$$3x + 5 = 6(x+4)$$

$3x + 5 = 6x + 24$ ← be careful here too!

ditch the 3x $\quad \underline{-3x \qquad\qquad -3x}$

$\qquad\qquad\qquad 5 = 3x + 24$

ditch the 24 $\quad \underline{-24 \qquad\qquad -24}$

$\qquad\qquad\qquad -19 = 3x$

ditch the 3 $\qquad \frac{-19}{3} = \frac{3x}{3}$

$\qquad\qquad\qquad \frac{-19}{3} = x$

Try it:

Solve $\quad \frac{2}{7}x - \frac{1}{2} = \frac{2}{3}(4x-1)$

* There are three guys to ditch!

Now for decimals... These are a snap!
If we want to solve this guy...

$$2.7x + 5 = 1.3$$

Let's clear out those decimals first!

$$2.7x + 5 = 1.3$$
$\quad\quad\uparrow \quad\quad\quad\uparrow$

There is <u>one</u> place behind each of the decimals... So, multiply both sides by 10!
$\quad\quad\quad\quad\quad\quad\quad\quad\quad\quad\quad\quad\quad\quad\uparrow$
$\quad\quad\quad\quad\quad\quad\quad\quad\quad\quad\quad\quad\quad$<u>one zero</u>

$$10(2.7x + 5) = 10(1.3)$$
$$27x + 50 = 13$$
$$\underline{\quad -50 \quad -50\quad} \quad\quad \text{ditch the 50}$$
$$27x = -37$$

$$\frac{27x}{27} = \frac{-37}{27} \quad \text{ditch the 27}$$

$$x = \frac{-37}{27}$$

Check out what's different about this guy:

$$6x - 2.59 = 7.3$$

↑ only one place here

two places here

we go for the max and multiply both sides by 100

↑↑ two zeros

$$100(6x - 2.59) = 100(7.3)$$

$$600x - 259 = 730$$

I'll let you finish it off:

Try it:

Solve $3.12x + 8 = 7.06 - 3.5x$

Solve $5 - 6.124x = 3.8$

Solving Equations - Dealing With Fractions & Decimals

Solving Inequalities - What Your Answers Will Look Like (Intervals)

For these problems, instead of just having one answer, like $x = 3$

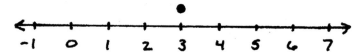

We are going to get a range of answers, called an interval... Like this:

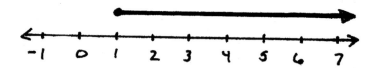

This means that x can be 1... or x can be bigger than 1... x can be 2 or 4.671 or 1.00001 or 50,000,000.

One way to write this interval is

$$x \geq 1$$

(read "x is greater than or equal to 1")

So, what would this mean on a number line?

$$x < 3$$

Just read it! "x is less than 3."

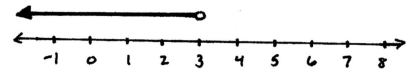

We put an open dot at the 3, since x cannot be 3.

So, $x < 3$ means that x cannot be 3, but it can be a number less than 3... like 2.998... or 0... or −5931.

Try it:

Graph $x > -2$ on a number line:

Graph $x \leq 5$ on a number line:

What about something like this?

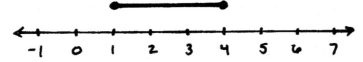

This means that x can be 1... or x can be 4... or x can be any number between 1 and 4... Like 2 or 3.01459.

One way to write this interval is

$$1 \leq x \leq 4$$

(read as "x is greater than or equal to 1 and less than or equal to 4")

So, how would we graph this on a number line?

$$-1 < x \leq 3$$

It says that x cannot be -1...

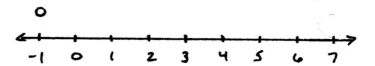

It says that x <u>can</u> be 3...

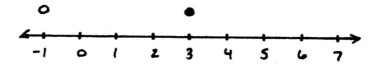

And it says that x can be a number between -1 and 3...

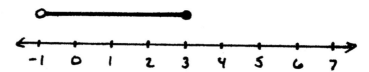

Your turn:

Graph $2 < x < 7$ on a number line:

Graph $-3 \leq x < 0$ on a number line:

What about something like this?

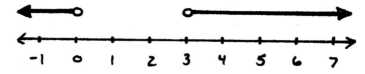

If you have to be just <u>one</u> x guy, you either have

to pick an x on the left side (in x<0) <u>or</u> an x on the right side (in x>3). Right?

So, we write it like this:

$$x < 0 \text{ \underline{or} } x > 3$$

All the guys we've been working with are called "inequalities" since they have the symbols $<, >, \leq, \geq$ instead of just $=$ signs.

Try one more:

Graph $x \leq -1$ or $x > 5$ on a number line:

Solving Inequalities - Set-Builder Notation

There are two notations for writing inequalities besides the basic style

$$0 \leq x < 4$$
$$x > -1$$
$$x \leq 2$$
$$x < 0 \text{ or } x > 3$$

The first one I'm going to show you is called "set-builder notation." All you have to do on this one is take the guys we have above and put them in a bracket thing like this:

$$\{ x \mid \underline{} \}$$

So, they'd be

$$\{ x \mid 0 \leq x < 4 \}$$
$$\{ x \mid x > -1 \}$$
$$\{ x \mid x \leq 2 \}$$
$$\{ x \mid x < 0 \text{ or } x > 3 \}$$

Here's how you read it and what it means:

$$\{ \} \leftarrow \text{This is set notation.}$$

You read the whole thing like...

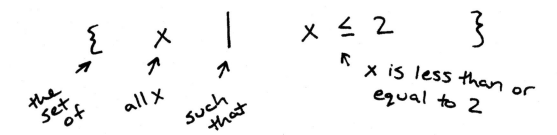

$\{ \quad x \quad | \quad x \leq 2 \quad \}$

the set of — all x — such that — x is less than or equal to 2

Personally, I think the next notation is a lot slicker... And the fact that I have an opinion on this makes me a royal geek. I'm aware!

Solving Inequalities - Interval Notation

This notation is my favorite for intervals. It's just a lot simpler!

Let's look at the intervals we did with the set-builder notation:

$$0 \leq x < 4$$
$$x > -1$$
$$x \leq 2$$
$$x < 0 \text{ or } x > 3$$

Let's start with the first one:

$$0 \leq x < 4$$

This is what it means:

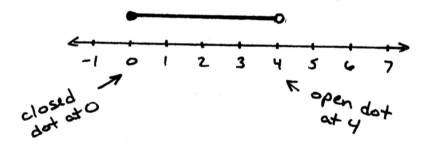

closed dot at 0 → open dot at 4

So, we write it like this:

$$[0, 4)$$ ← This is interval notation!

Use [or] for closed dots → $\leq, \geq$

Use (or) for open dots → $<, >$

So,

$-7 < x < 10$ would be $(-7, 10)$
and
$3 < x \leq 205$ would be $(3, 205]$

Easy!

Try it:

Write the interval notation for:

$2 \leq x < 5$

$0 \leq x \leq 7$

$-6 < x < 4$

$-10 < x < 0$

What about $x > -1$?

Here it is on the number line:

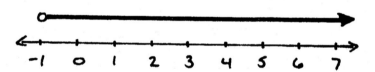

x can't be -1, but it can be greater than -1... It can be 2... or $5,397,241$.

These go on forever, so we write

$$(-1, \infty)$$

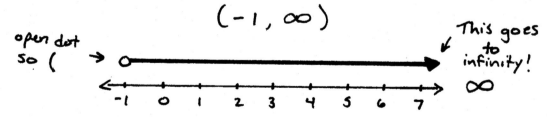

open dot so (

This goes to infinity! ∞

Here's another one:
$$x \leq 2$$
Here's the number line:

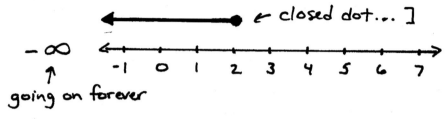

The interval notation is
$$(-\infty, 2]$$

We use a parenthesis here since we can't actually equal infinity.

One important thing here:

Notice that we put the $-\infty$ on the left because you always put the guys in order from left to right as they appear on the number line.

Your turn:

Write the interval notation for

$x \geq 2$

$x < 4$

$x > 0$

$x \leq -3$

What about those two-piece guys?

```
←────o        o────────→
←─┼──┼──┼──┼──┼──┼──┼──┼──┼→
-∞  -1  0  1  2  3  4  5  6  7  ∞
```

The left piece is $(-\infty, 0)$.   The right piece is $(3, \infty)$.

Remember the regular notation:

$$x < 0 \text{ or } x > 3$$

↑ We have to deal with the "or."

Remember way back when you learned sets?

"or" means "union" and we use "∪"

So, the interval notation is

$$(-\infty, 0) \cup (3, \infty)$$

Try it:

Write the interval notation for

$x \leq -5$ or $x > 0$

$x \leq 3$ or $x \geq 10$

$x < 0$ or $x > 2$

I'll be using interval notation in the rest of the lessons.

Solving Inequalities - Solving Basic Guys

Let's jump in and try one!

Solve $2x - 5 \geq 7$

Hmm... Well, we know how to solve

$$2x - 5 = 7$$

Right? Guess what? We do it the same way!

* There's only one freaky thing you'll have to watch out for and it's in the next lesson.

Here we go:

$$2x - 5 \geq 7$$
$$\underline{+5 \quad +5} \quad \text{ditch the 5}$$
$$2x \geq 12$$
$$\frac{2x}{2} \geq \frac{12}{2} \quad \text{ditch the 2}$$
$$x \geq 6$$

OK, so what does this answer mean?
(It's super important in math to understand what your answers mean!)

We can graph it on a number line:

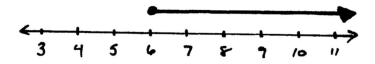

So, in our original problem, $2x - 5 \geq 7$,

x can be 6... or x can be a number bigger than 6.

Try sticking some numbers in!

$$2x - 5 \geq 7$$

$x = 6 \rightarrow \quad 2(6) - 5 \geq 7$
$\qquad\qquad\qquad 7 \geq 7 \quad$ Yep - that's true!

$x = 10 \rightarrow \quad 2(10) - 5 \geq 7$
$\qquad\qquad\qquad 15 \geq 7 \quad$ Yep - that's true!

What about something less than 6?

$x = 2 \rightarrow \quad 2(2) - 5 \geq 7$
$\qquad\qquad\qquad -1 \geq 7 \quad$ __FALSE!__

So, any number that is 6 or bigger works in the inequality.

In interval notation, our answer is

$$[6, \infty)$$

Here's another one:

$$3x + 2 < x - 4$$

Pretend it's $3x + 2 = x - 4$ and go for it!

$$\begin{array}{r} 3x + 2 < x - 4 \\ -x \qquad -x \\ \hline 2x + 2 < -4 \end{array}$$ ditch the smaller x guy

---

Solving Inequalities - Solving Basic Guys

$$2x + 2 < -4$$
$$\underline{-2-2}\text{ditch the 2}$$
$$2x < -6$$
$$\frac{2x}{2} < \frac{-6}{2}\text{ditch the 2}$$
$$x < -3$$

This means that all numbers less than 3 will work in the original problem:

$$3x + 2 < x - 4$$

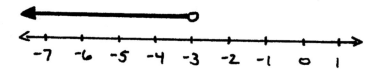

Try sticking some numbers in:

$x = -10 \rightarrow 3(-10) + 2 < -10 - 4$
$ -28 < -14 $ Yep!

$x = 50 \rightarrow 3(50) + 2 < 50 - 4$
$ 152 < 46 $ NOPE!

$x = -3 \rightarrow 3(-3) + 2 < -3 - 4$
$ -7 < -7 $ NOPE!

So, the answer in interval notation is:

$$(-\infty, -3)$$

It's definitely a good idea to try some numbers to make sure you've got that arrow pointing in the right direction. This will save your caboose in the next section a<u>nd</u> on tests!

Your turn:

* and remember to always ditch the smaller x guy first!

Solve $\qquad 8x - 3 \leq 13$

Solve $\qquad 10x - 7 > 4x + 35$

Solving Inequalities - The Freaky Thing

Check this one out:

Solve $-3x \leq 6$

$$\frac{-3x}{-3} \leq \frac{6}{-3} \qquad \text{ditch the -3}$$

$$x \leq -2$$

It <u>looks</u> ok... But, is it?

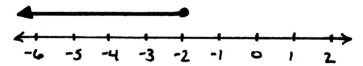

This means that x can be -2 or any number less than -2.

Let's check!

$$-3x \leq 6$$

$x = -2 \rightarrow \quad -3(-2) \leq 6$
$\qquad\qquad\quad 6 \leq 6 \quad$ Yep - that works.

$x = -4 \rightarrow \quad -3(-4) \leq 6$
$\qquad\qquad\quad 12 \leq 6 \quad$ NO WAY, DUDE!

It didn't work. Wazzup with that?

Here's the freaky thing:

> When you divide (or multiply) by a negative number, you mess up the inequality sign!

But, it's easy to fix!

> When you multiply or divide an inequality by a negative number, FLIP THE SIGN!

Let's try it:

$$-3x \leq 6$$

$$\frac{-3x}{-3} \geq \frac{6}{-3} \quad \text{alert!} \\ \text{divide by } -3 \text{ and flip the sign}$$

$$x \geq -2$$

check it:

$x = -2 \rightarrow$ We already know this works because of the equals (=) part.

$x = 0 \rightarrow$
$$-3(0) \leq 6$$
$$0 \leq 6 \quad \text{Yep!}$$

$x = -10 \rightarrow$
$$-3(-10) \leq 6$$
$$30 \leq 6 \quad \text{NOPE!}$$

ok, we have it now!

$$[-2, \infty)$$

Try it:
$$-4x > 20$$

This is why, when we've got something like
$$3x + 2 < x - 4$$
I always tell you to ditch the smaller x guy first! See what happens if we start by ditching the $3x$ instead:

$$
\begin{array}{r}
3x + 2 < x - 4 \\
-3x \phantom{+2<} -3x \\
\hline
2 < -2x - 4 \\
+4 \phantom{<-2x} +4 \\
\hline
\end{array}
$$

DANGER! → $6 < -2x$

Now, we'd have to divide by a negative... And, if we forget to flip the sign, we're dead. Trust me, I've graded thousands of these problems and even the best students forget to flip signs when they are nervous. It's best to avoid it if you can — just one less thing to worry about!

One other important thing -- and this one is common...

You only flip the sign when dividing <u>by</u> a negative number... Not when you are dividing <u>into</u> a negative number!

When you do it: $-5x < 10$

$$\frac{-5x}{-5} > \frac{10}{-5} \text{ alert!}$$

When you don't do it: $4x \geq -8$

$$\frac{4x}{4} \geq \frac{-8}{4} \text{ ok}$$

Your turn:

$$-10x < 30$$

$$5 - 7x \geq 33$$

Solving Inequalities — The Freaky Thing

Solving Inequalities - Compound Inequalities

So far, we've just been solving inequalities with two parts: a left side and a right side like this

$$5x > 2x - 7$$

But, sometimes we'll have inequalities with three parts:

$$-3 \leq 2x - 1 \leq 5$$

Sometimes, these are called compound inequalities.

So, what do we do on these?

Our goal is the same:

> **Get the x alone!**

On these, we just get him alone in the middle section. So, just like before, pretend that there are really = signs and go about your business... We'll just be working all three sections at once.

Let's go:

$$-3 \leq 2x - 1 \leq 5$$

Get the x alone in the middle...

$$-3 \leq 2x - 1 \leq 5 \quad \text{ditch the } -1$$
$$+1 \qquad +1 \quad +1$$
$$\overline{-2 \leq 2x \leq 6}$$

$$-2 \le 2x \le 6$$

ditch the 2

$$\frac{-2}{2} \le \frac{2x}{2} \le \frac{6}{2}$$

$$-1 \le x \le 3$$

<--+--+--+--●━━━━━━━●--+--+-->
-3 -2 -1 0 1 2 3 4 5

$$[-1, 3]$$

But, what does this mean?

x can be -1... or x can be 3... or x can be a number between -1 and 3... like 0 or 2.315.

Check it:

$$-3 \le 2x - 1 \le 5$$

$x = -1 \rightarrow$ $\quad -3 \le 2(-1) - 1 \le 5$
$\quad\quad\quad\quad\quad -3 \le -3 \le 5 \quad$ Yep!

$x = 3 \rightarrow$ $\quad -3 \le 2(3) - 1 \le 5$
$\quad\quad\quad\quad\quad -3 \le 5 \le 5 \quad$ Yep!

$x = 0 \rightarrow$ $\quad -3 \le 2(0) - 1 \le 5$
$\quad\quad\quad\quad\quad -3 \le -1 \le 5 \quad$ Yep!

$x = 100 \rightarrow$ $\quad -3 \le 2(100) - 1 \le 5$
$\quad\quad\quad\quad\quad -3 \le 199 \le 5 \quad$ NOPE!

Try it:
$$-5 < 3x+1 \leq 10$$

$$0 \leq 5x-2 \leq 7$$

ARE YOU TOTALLY STRESSED OUT?

You don't have to feel out of control. You don't have to feel nervous. You don't have to feel tired and foggy all the time. Believe me, I've been there myself. I totally remember what it was like to be a student -- and I was a student for a LONG time! Since then, I've been a college teacher so I'm around students all the time - most of them stressed out. Over the years, I've been teaching my students how to de-stress and how to deal with stress... I finally decided to make a stress management site specially designed FOR students -- and anyone else who feels stressed out.

So, settle down and KNOW that you CAN lower your stress! You really ARE in control of what's going on in your world! YOU CAN ACTUALLY BE HAPPY AND RELAXED -- yeah, even while you're a student!

TotallyStressedOut.com
The stress management site for students

Are you already in credit card trouble?
Is your FICO score the pits?
Uh... FICO who?
Do you want to learn about this stuff?

Do you want to learn how to be SMART & RICH?

financeFREAK.com

A fool and his money are soon parted.
Don't be a fool... Be a FREAK!

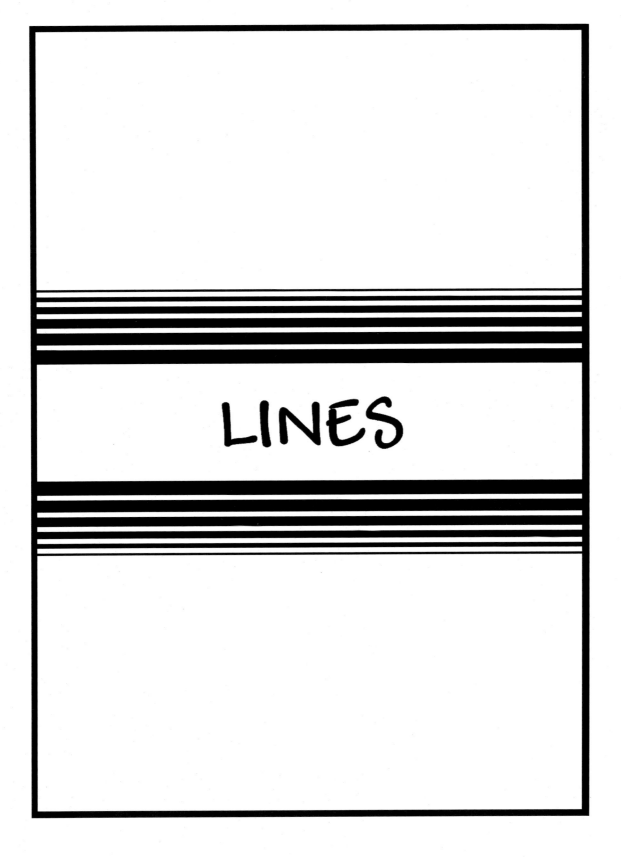

Lines - The Rectangular Coordinate System

This is just a grid that you'll be drawing all sorts of cool math things on -- like lines.

Remember our old number line?

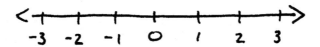

Well, now we're going to do this in two directions -- make that two dimensions! Check it out:

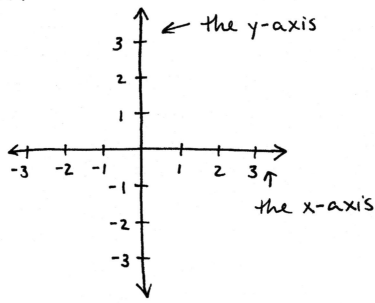

Think of it as a floor -- a two dimensional plane that you can draw on.

Lines - Plotting Points

Whenever we draw a point on our grid, we'll call it "plotting a point."

The grid is really called a "graph" and the points we plot are called "coordinates." These are really locations on the plane -- we're just finding and labeling them.

Coordinates are just ordered pairs of numbers like

$$(3,2) \text{ or } (0,-5) \text{ or } (\tfrac{1}{2}, 6)$$

(Be sure not to confuse this with interval notation -- it may look the same, but, it's a totally different thing.)

Coordinates always follow this order:

$$(x, y)$$

It's alphabetical!

So, $(3,2)$ means that $x=3$ and $y=2$...

$(0,-5)$ means $x=0$ and $y=-5$...

$(\tfrac{1}{2}, 6)$ means $x=\tfrac{1}{2}$ and $y=6$.

Let's plot (3,2)... x = 3...
So, we'll go over to positive 3 on the x-axis...

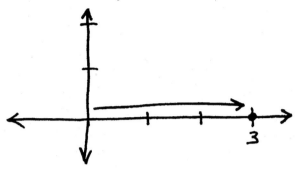

and y = 2...
So, we'll go up 2 (the positive direction) in the y direction...

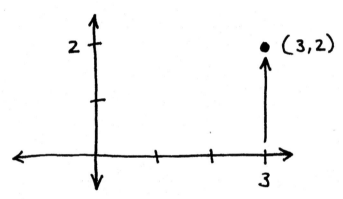

What about (0,-5)?

x = 0... So, we don't go anywhere in the x direction...

y = -5...

So, we go down 5 (because it's negative) in the y direction...

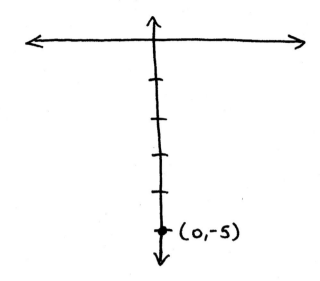

Here are a bunch of other points on the graph:

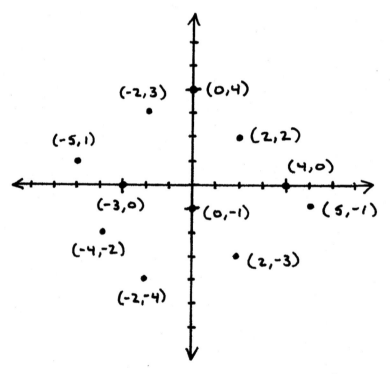

The point (0,0) is special. It's called the origin.

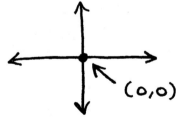

LINES

Lines - Graphing Lines Using Intercepts

There are two efficient and accepted methods for graphing lines -- this is one of them. For the other one, we'll need some more ammunition, so I'll save it for later. You will need to master both.

On to method 1... First of all, you'll need to know what an intercept is!

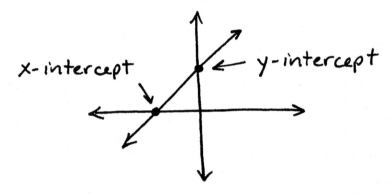

The intercepts are where a graph crosses the x and y axes.

Not only are these the easiest points to find, as you'll see later in math, they are the most important points.

Here's how this works... Let's graph

$$3x - y = 6$$

Make an xy table:

x	y

Fill in 0's for the x and y like this:

x	y
0	
	0

Let's look at the first one:

x	y
0	
	0

← When x=0 we have →

$3x - y = 6$
$3(0) - y = 6$
$-y = 6$
$y = -6$

The easiest thing to do is to just cover up the 3x part with your finger:

🖐 $- y = 6$

So, we get

x	y
0	-6

← (0,-6) is a point on our graph -- the y-intercept.

232   LINES   232

Now, let's look at the second one:

x	y
0	-6
	0

← When $y=0$ we have →

$3x - y = 6$
$3x - 0 = 6$
$3x = 6$
$x = 2$

Just cover the y guy with your finger:

$3x \;\fbox{}\; = 6$

So, we get

x	y
0	-6
2	0

← (2,0) is a point on our graph -- the x-intercept.

Since we just need two points to draw the line, we're set!

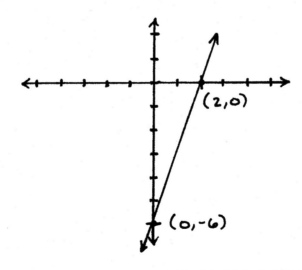

Here's another one:

$$\text{Graph } x + 2y = 4$$

①
x	y
0	
	0

→ ② (0) + 2y = 4
      y = 2

---

③
x	y
0	2
	0

→ ④ x(0) = 4
      x = 4

---

⑤
x	y
0	2
4	0

⑥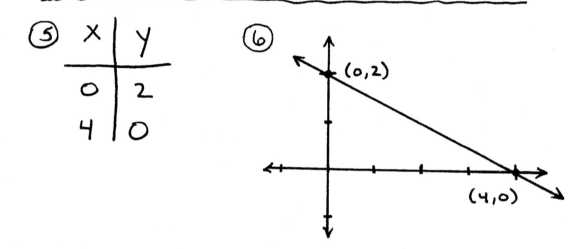
(0,2)
(4,0)

Always label the two points on your graph! Why? Three reasons:
    a) Your teacher will require it.
    b) It's polite.
    c) If your drawing skills...uh... stink, at least your teacher will know what you meant!

Sometimes I call this the "finger cover-up method."

Try it:

Graph $x - y = 3$ by finding the intercepts.

Graph $-3x + 4y = 12$ by finding the intercepts.

Lines - What's the Slope of a Line?

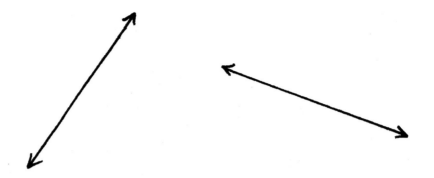

These lines look pretty different, don't they? Lines are used to keep track of lots of info -- like how much money a company makes. Just off the top of your head, which of the lines above would you want to describe the profits of your company? Whether the line is tilted up or down all of the sudden gets really important!

I am now going to introduce you to

    Pierre the Mountain Climbing Ant

    (He's kind of a pathetic math super hero.)

For slopes, Pierre is going to walk on the lines from left to right -- just like we read.

On these lines, Pierre is climbing UPHILL.

Uphill slopes are positive slopes -- the slope will be a positive number like 5 or $\frac{2}{3}$.

On these lines, Pierre is climbing DOWNHILL!

Downhill slopes are negative slopes -- the slope will be a negative number like -7 or $-\frac{1}{3}$.

There are three ways to find the slope of a line. Two of them are in the next two lessons and the third will come later.

Lines - Finding the Slope of a Line from the Graph

Let's look at the line going through the points $(-2,-1)$ and $(4,3)$

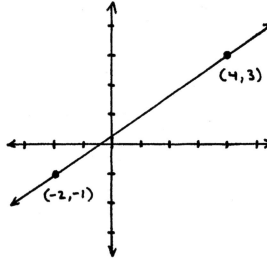

The simplest way to look at the slope is

$$\frac{rise}{run}$$

(rise over run)

To get from the point $(-2,-1)$ to the point $(4,3)$, you rise up 4... and run over 6.

The slope is

$$\frac{rise}{run} = \frac{4}{6} = \frac{2}{3}$$

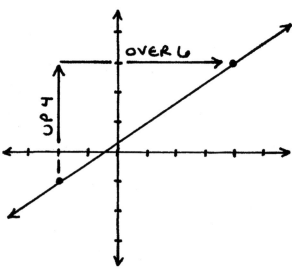

* Notice that the slope goes uphill and $\frac{2}{3}$ is a positive number.

For $\frac{rise}{run}$, you can "rise" up or down... but, you always "run" to the right. ALWAYS!

$$\frac{rise \updownarrow}{run \rightarrow}$$

Check it out:
Let's find the slope of this line:

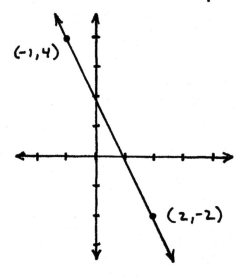
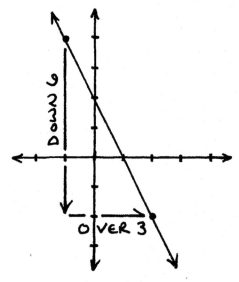

$$slope = \frac{rise}{run} = \frac{-6}{3} = -2$$

Negative -- and the line is going downhill.

Lines - Finding the Slope of a Line From the Graph

Your turn:
   Graph the line that passes through the points
        (0, -3) and (5, 4)
Then, use the graph to find the slope.

Lines - Finding the Slope of a Line From Two Points

Let's use the examples in the last lesson... We'll use the first one to find a formula.

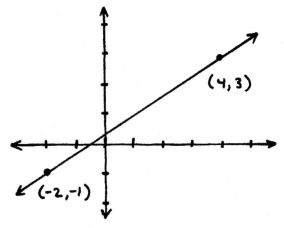

We'll use the letter m for slope.

$$m = \frac{rise}{run}$$

Look at $\frac{rise}{run}$ as

$$\frac{\text{the change in the y's}}{\text{the change in the x's}}$$

$$= \frac{3-(-1)}{4-(-2)} = \frac{4}{6} = \frac{2}{3}$$

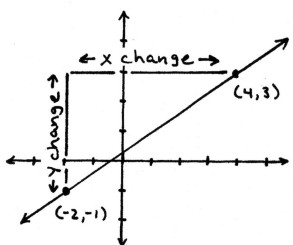

Here's the official formula:

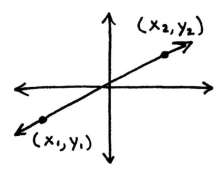

If you're given two points (x_1, y_1) and (x_2, y_2)

$$m = \frac{y_2 - y_1}{x_2 - x_1}$$

So, in our last example...

$(-2, -1) \quad\quad (4, 3)$
$x_1 y_1 \quad\quad x_2 y_2$

$$m = \frac{y_2 - y_1}{x_2 - x_1} = \frac{3 - (-1)}{4 - (-2)} = \frac{4}{6} = \frac{2}{3}$$

<u>But</u>, notice something cool...

The order of the points doesn't matter! Let's switch them and see what we get:

$(4, 3) \quad\quad (-2, -1)$
$x_1 y_1 \quad\quad x_2 y_2$

$$m = \frac{y_2 - y_1}{x_2 - x_1} = \frac{-1 - 3}{-2 - 4} = \frac{-4}{-6} = \frac{2}{3}$$

↗ Same thing!

Let's try our new formula with the second example in the last lesson:

It was the line passing through
$(-1, 4)$ and $(2, -2)$

$$m = \frac{y_2 - y_1}{x_2 - x_1} = \frac{-2 - 4}{2 - (-1)} = \frac{-6}{3} = -2$$

Your turn:

Without graphing, find the slope of the line that passes through the points

(0, -3) and (5, 4)

Lines - Equations of Lines (Graphing Method 2)

There are two forms used for equations of lines. This is the one we've already seen and learned to graph:

> **FORM 1: General (standard)**
>
> $$Ax + By = C$$

example: $2x - 3y = 6$

Remember that you graph this guy by finding the intercepts!
Do it, baby!

Here's the new one:

> **FORM 2: Slope-intercept (or y-intercept)**
>
> $$y = mx + b$$

This form is my favorite because, if you know what the pieces are, it's <u>super</u> easy to graph!

Here are the pieces:

$$y = mx + b$$

↗ slope   ↑ y-intercept

Check it out:

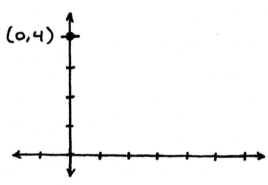

Graph $y = \frac{-3}{5}x + 4$

① It crosses the y-axis at 4, so we start there:

② the slope is $\frac{-3}{5}$... so we

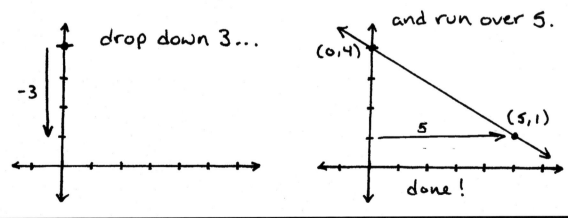

drop down 3...   and run over 5.

done!

245 Lines - Equations of Lines (Graphing Method 2) 245

Let's do another one:

Graph $y = 4x - 2$

① It crosses the y-axis at $y = -2$, so we start there:

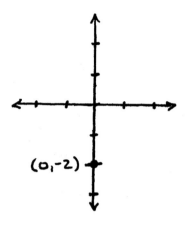
(0,-2)

② The slope is 4 which is really $\frac{4}{1}$...

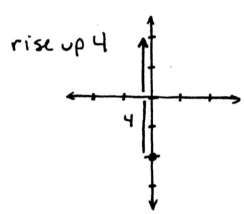
rise up 4

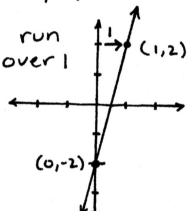
run over 1
(1,2)
(0,-2)

Your turn:

Graph $y = \frac{1}{2}x - 3$

Lines - Horizontal & Vertical Lines

What if we want to graph this?

$$y = -2$$

Hmm... It doesn't look like there's enough there! Where's the x? We're used to these:

$$Ax + By = C \quad \text{and} \quad y = mx + b$$

Well, here's the deal:

If the x isn't there, then it can be anything! And y is locked in at -2.

So, what would this look like?

It's a horizontal line!

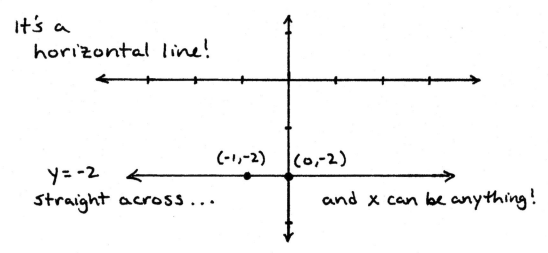

$y = -2$ straight across...   and x can be anything!

$(-1, -2)$ $(0, -2)$

So, what's the slope of this line? Grab two points and see?

$$m = \frac{y_2 - y_1}{x_2 - x_1} = \frac{-2 - (-2)}{-1 - 0} = \frac{0}{-1} = 0$$

The slope of a horizontal line is 0!

Since it's always hard to remember when these guys are horizontal and when they are vertical, I've got a sentence that will always save you...

When you see $y = -2$, say this:

| Y is always -2 and x can be anything! |

This tells you what the graph should look like!

Try it:

Graph $y = 1$ ... Then, grab two points and find the slope.

Now, let's graph this thing:

$$x = 3$$

Dang! That's even weirder than the last guy!

Let's use what we've learned...

If y isn't there, then it can be anything!

And x is locked in at 3.

What's your sentence?

> X is always 3...
> and y can be anything!

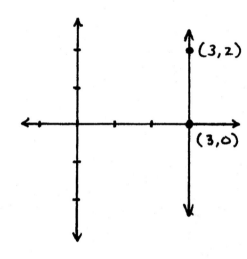

It's a vertical line!
What's the slope?

$$m = \frac{2-0}{3-3} = \frac{2}{0}$$

The slope of a vertical line is undefined.

This is the official word.

Your turn:

Graph $x = -4$, then grab two points and find the slope.

Lines - Graphing Overview

Here's what we've learned so far about graphing lines:

① If it's in the form
$$Ax + By = C$$
graph it by finding the intercepts.

② If it's in the form
$$y = mx + b$$
start at $y = b$ and, then, use the slope (rise over run) to nail the second point.

③ If it's in the form
$$y = \#$$
then it's a horizontal line.

④ If it's in the form
$$x = \#$$
then it's a vertical line.

Do all the problems on the next page, then there's one glitch I need to tell you about.

Graph $5x + 2y = -10$

Graph $y = -2x + 3$

Graph $y = 4$

Graph $x = 4$

Lines – Graphing Overview

OK, here's the glitch:
Let's try to graph this:
$$2x - 3y = 0$$

Well, it's form 1: $Ax + By = C$ ...
Let's go for the intercepts...

x	y
0	
	0

→ $(0) - 3y = 0$
$y = 0$ →

x	y
0	0

---

x	y
0	0
	0

→ $2x(0) = 0$
$x = 0$ →

x	y
0	0
0	0

Not very helpful, was it?
We have **one** point on our graph:

(0,0)

$2x - 3y = 0$ ← This 0 is the problem!
So, what do we do?

252 LINES 252

Let's change it to form 2! $y = mx + b$
Check it out:

$$2x - 3y = 0 \quad \text{get the y alone}$$
$$\underline{-2x \qquad\quad -2x}$$
$$-3y = -2x \qquad \div -3$$
$$\frac{-3y}{-3} = \frac{-2x}{-3}$$
$$y = \frac{-2}{-3}x$$
$$y = \frac{2}{3}x$$

Well, it almost looks like $y = mx + b$...
How about this?

$$y = \frac{2}{3}x + 0$$

Now, <u>this</u> I can graph!

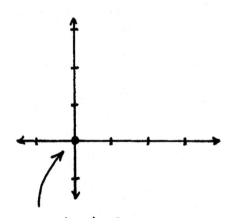

start at 0...
which we already had...

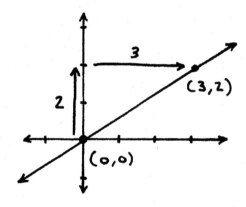

Lines - Graphing Overview

Your turn:
Graph $x + 4y = 0$

Lines - Finding the Slope From the Equation of a Line

This is going to be a lot like what we just did at the end of the last section.

So far, I've shown you how to find the slope from the graph and when you have two points...

But, what if you just have the equation?

If it's like this guy, then it's a snap!

$$y = \frac{7}{2}x - 3$$

Since it's in $y = mx + b$ form, we can easily see that the slope is $\frac{7}{2}$.

So, what if it's in standard form like this?

$$2x + y = 5$$

Well, it's not too bad. We just do a little algebra and get it into $y = mx + b$ form.

To do this, we solve for y:

$$2x + y = 5$$
$$\underline{-2x \qquad -2x}$$
$$y = -2x + 5$$

The slope is -2.

Try it:
  Find the slope using algebra:
  $$-3x + y = 7$$

Here's another one:
$$5x - y = 2$$

Solve for y:

$$5x - y = 2$$
$$\underline{-5x \qquad -5x}$$
$$-y = -5x + 2 \qquad \text{multiply by } -1$$
$$y = 5x - 2$$

The slope is 5.

They just get a little messier:
$$5x - 3y = 2$$

Solve for y:

$$5x - 3y = 2$$
$$\underline{-5x \qquad -5x}$$
$$-3y = -5x + 2$$

$$\frac{-3y}{-3} = \frac{-5x+2}{-3} \qquad \div -3$$

$$y = \frac{-5x}{-3} + \frac{2}{-3}$$

$$y = \frac{5}{3}x - \frac{2}{3}$$

The slope is $\frac{5}{3}$.

Your turn:

Find the slope using algebra:

$$7x + 2y = -3$$

Lines - Finding the Equation of a Line Given a Point and a Slope

If we have a point, (x_1, y_1), and a slope, m, here's the formula we use to find the equation of a line:

$$\boxed{y - y_1 = m(x - x_1)}$$

It's called the point-slope formula. (Duh!)

You are going to use this a LOT!

Luckily, it's pretty easy -- let's just do one:

Let's find the equation of the line that passes through the point $(4, -3)$ with a slope of -2:

$$y - y_1 = m(x - x_1)$$

$m = -2 \qquad (4, -3)$
$\qquad\qquad\quad\, x_1 \;\; y_1$

Just stick the stuff in and clean it up!

$$y - (-3) = -2(x - 4)$$
$$y + 3 = -2x + 8 \;\; \leftarrow \text{be careful here!}$$
$$\underline{\;-3 \qquad\qquad -3}$$
$$y = -2x + 5 \qquad \text{done}$$

Try it:

Find the equation of the line that passes through the point $(-2, 6)$ with a slope of 3:

Here's a messier one -- there's something to really watch out for on the clean up!

Let's find the equation of the line that passes through the point $(-5, 2)$ with a slope of $-\frac{3}{4}$.

$$y - y_1 = m(x - x_1)$$

$$y - 2 = -\frac{3}{4}(x - (-5))$$

To clean this up, we'll multiply both sides by 4:

$$4(y-2) = 4\left(-\frac{3}{4}\right)(x+5)$$

Be very careful here! You only multiply the 4 into the guy in front!

$$4y - 8 = -3(x+5)$$

$$4y - 8 = -3x - 15$$
$$+8 +8$$
$$4y = -3x - 7$$

$4y = -3x - 7$
$+3x +3x$
$3x + 4y = -7$

OR

$\dfrac{4y}{4} = \dfrac{-3x - 7}{4}$

$y = -\dfrac{3}{4}x - \dfrac{7}{4}$

(Depending on what form you want.)

Your turn:

Find the equation of the line that passes through the point $(1, -8)$ with a slope of $\dfrac{2}{5}$.

---

260   LINES   260

Lines - Finding the Equation of a Line Given Two Points

In the last lesson, I showed you how to get the equation of a line given a point and a slope using the formula

$$y - y_1 = m(x - x_1)$$

Anytime we need to get the equation of a line, we need two things

① a point   ② a slope

ALWAYS!

So, what do we do if we are just given two points and no slope?

No problem -- we'll just use the two points to pop the slope using this guy:

$$m = \frac{y_2 - y_1}{x_2 - x_1}$$

Check it out:

Let's find the equation of the line that passes through the points

$$(1, 3) \text{ and } (-2, 5)$$

This one's a two-stepper...

STEP 1: Find the slope

$$m = \frac{y_2 - y_1}{x_2 - x_1} = \frac{5-3}{-2-1} = \frac{2}{-3} = \frac{-2}{3}$$

STEP 2: Now, use the point-slope formula with one of our points, $(1, 3)$, and $m = \frac{-2}{3}$

* I picked $(1, 3)$ since it didn't have any negatives -- it's just easier.

$$y - y_1 = m(x - x_1)$$
$$y - 3 = \frac{-2}{3}(x - 1) \quad \text{multiply by 3}$$
$$3(y-3) = 3\left(\frac{-2}{3}\right)(x-1)$$
$$3y - 9 = -2(x-1)$$
$$3y - 9 = -2x + 2$$
$$\underline{+9 \qquad\qquad +9}$$
$$3y = -2x + 11$$

$2x + 3y = 11$ \qquad or \qquad $y = \frac{-2}{3}x + \frac{11}{3}$

Your turn:

Find the equation of the line passing through the points $(-4, 5)$ and $(2, -3)$.

Lines - Parallel Lines

This is easy! Look at these parallel lines:

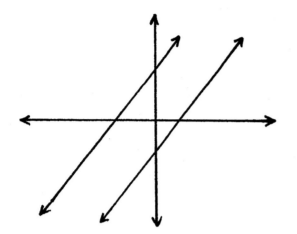

What do they have in common?

> The same slope!

So, two lines are parallel if they have the same slope.

The problems in this section (and the next) are cool because they pull together a bunch of stuff I've shown you.

Check it out:

Let's find the equation of the line that passes through the point $(-3, 5)$ and is parallel to the line $2y - 4x = 1$.

* To get the equation of a line we need:
   ① a point -- which we have
   ② a slope -- which we can get from $2y - 4x = 1$ (since they are parallel, they'll have the same slope.)

STEP 1: Find the slope

$$2y - 4x = 1$$
$$+4x +4x$$
$$2y = 4x + 1$$
$$\frac{2y}{2} = \frac{4x+1}{2}$$
$$y = 2x + \frac{1}{2}$$

Get it in $y = mx + b$ form. So, solve for y.

slope = 2

STEP 2: Use the point-slope form with the point $(-3, 5)$ and the slope of 2

$$y - y_1 = m(x - x_1)$$
$$y - 5 = 2(x - (-3))$$
$$y - 5 = 2(x + 3)$$
$$y - 5 = 2x + 6$$
$$y = 2x + 11 \quad \text{Done!}$$

I'll let you check our answer by graphing both lines to see if they are really parallel!

Graph $2y - 4x = 1$
and $y = 2x + 11$ on
the same graph:

Lines - Parallel Lines

Your turn:

Find the equation of the line that passes through the point $(1,-2)$ and is parallel to the line $3x + 5y = -1$.

Lines - Perpendicular Lines

Let's graph these lines:

$$y = 2x \quad \text{and} \quad y = -\tfrac{1}{2}x$$

* I'm using $y = mx + b$ stuff to graph them!

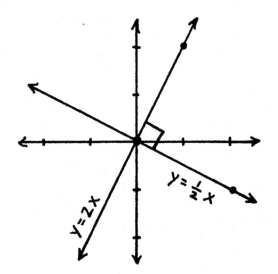

These lines are perpendicular.

(They form a 90° angle.)

So, what's going on with the slopes?

$$m_1 = 2 \text{ and } m_2 = -\tfrac{1}{2}$$

Notice that they are inverses but the signs are different.

A typical math book would say:

$$m_1 \cdot m_2 = (2)\left(-\tfrac{1}{2}\right) = -1$$

But this is easier:

You flip it over and change the sign -- that's how you get the slopes of perpendicular lines.

* If you want to be a super geek, you can rap it!

Check it out:

$$m_1 = 2 \text{ and } m_2 = \frac{-1}{2}$$

Take the 2... write it as a fraction: $\frac{2}{1}$

Flip it over: $\frac{1}{2}$ ... and change the sign: $\frac{-1}{2}$

Let's do a problem:

Let's find the equation of the line that passes through the point $(1, 3)$ and is perpendicular to the line $2x + 5y = 4$.

What do we need?

a point (have)   a slope (need)

STEP 1: Find the slope

It's perpendicular to $2x + 5y = 4$...
So, we'll get this guy's slope...
flip it and change the sign! Easy!

$$2x + 5y = 4$$
$$-2x \qquad\qquad -2x$$
$$5y = -2x + 4$$
$$y = \frac{-2}{5}x + 4$$

m_1 ↗   So, use $m_2 = \frac{5}{2}$

---

268   LINES   268

STEP 2: Use the point-slope formula with $(1,3)$ and $m = \frac{5}{2}$

$$y - y_1 = m(x - x_1)$$
$$y - 3 = \frac{5}{2}(x - 1) \quad \text{multiply by 2}$$
$$2(y - 3) = 2\left(\frac{5}{2}\right)(x - 1)$$
$$2y - 6 = 5(x - 1)$$
$$2y - 6 = 5x - 5$$
$$\underline{+6 \qquad +6}$$
$$2y = 5x + 1$$
$$y = \frac{5}{2}x + \frac{1}{2}$$

Graph

$$2x + 5y = 4$$

and

$$y = \frac{5}{2}x + \frac{1}{2}$$

and see if they really look perpendicular.

Try it:

Find the equation of the line that passes through the point (-2, 2) and is perpendicular to the line $3x - y = 1$.

Lines - Graphing Line Inequalities

OK, now you're an expert at graphing lines like

$$x + y = 3$$

But, what if we stick an inequality in there?

$$x + y \leq 3$$

Don't worry. If you use your head, it's not that bad. It's just one more thing to worry about.

Let's graph the line:

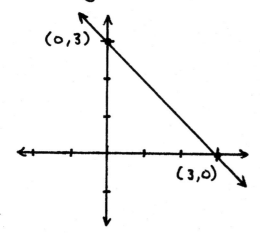

This takes care of the $x + y = 3$ part...

So, what about the $\leq$?

Remember that this rectangular coordinate grid is just made up of a bunch of (x,y) points.

All the points <u>on</u> the line work in this part:

$$x + y = 3$$

Now, we just need to find all the points that work in this part:

$$x + y < 3$$

Here's how we find these points:
We just pick a point off the line and test it!

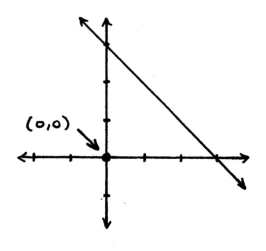

The origin, (0,0), is really easy to work with, so let's try it:

$$x + y < 3$$
$$0 + 0 < 3$$
$$0 < 3$$

(0,0) works in $x+y<3$!

Here's the deal: If (0,0) works, then all the points on the same side of the line will work. Don't believe me? Let's try a couple more:

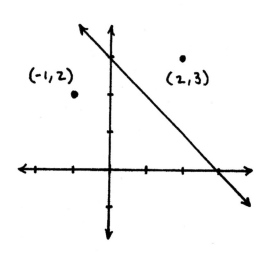

(-1,2): $x + y < 3$
         $-1 + 2 < 3$
         $1 < 3$ yep!

___

(2,3): $x + y < 3$
        $2 + 3 < 3$
        $5 < 3$ nope!

So, our answer is this:

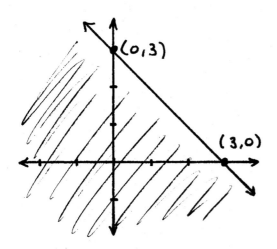

All the (x,y) points on the line and in the shaded region work in

$$x + y \leq 3$$

Here's another one:

Graph $2x + y > 4$

① Do the line:

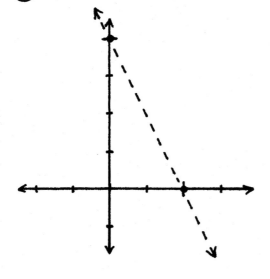

We make it a dashed line since there is no $=$.

So, which side do we shade?

Let's try $(0,0)$:

$$2x + y > 4$$
$$2(0) + 0 > 4$$
$$0 > 4 \quad \text{Nope!}$$

$(0,0)$ doesn't work! That means nothing on that side will work... So, all the good points must be on the other side!

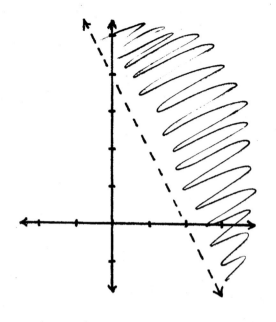

All the points in the shaded region work in

$$2x + y > 4$$

Try it:

Graph $x + y > -2$

This one's a little harder:

Graph $y > \frac{1}{3}x$

* Remember -- to graph this guy use $y = mx + b$. And we'll use a dashed line since there is no $=$.

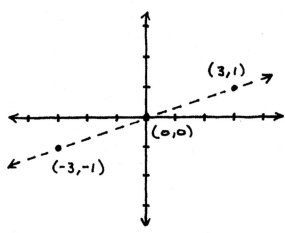

What side do we shade? The only glitch on this one is that we can't try (0,0) because it's <u>on</u> the line.

Let's try (1,2):

$$y > \tfrac{1}{3} x$$

$$2 > \tfrac{1}{3}(1)$$

$$2 > \tfrac{1}{3}$$

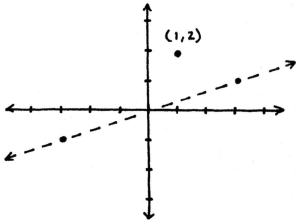

Yep! It works! So, shade that side:

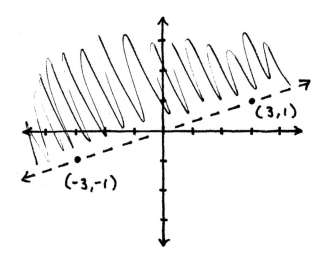

All the (x,y) points in the shaded region work in

$$y > \tfrac{1}{3} x$$

Your turn:
  Graph $y \leq 2x$

LINES

Are you already in credit card trouble?
Is your FICO score the pits?
Uh... FICO who?
Do you want to learn about this stuff?

> Do you want to learn how to be SMART & RICH?

financeFREAK.com

A fool and his money are soon parted.
Don't be a fool... Be a FREAK!

ARE YOU TOTALLY STRESSED OUT?

You don't have to feel out of control. You don't have to feel nervous. You don't have to feel tired and foggy all the time. Believe me, I've been there myself. I totally remember what it was like to be a student -- and I was a student for a LONG time! Since then, I've been a college teacher so I'm around students all the time - most of them stressed out. Over the years, I've been teaching my students how to de-stress and how to deal with stress... I finally decided to make a stress management site specially designed FOR students -- and anyone else who feels stressed out.

So, settle down and KNOW that you CAN lower your stress! You really ARE in control of what's going on in your world! YOU CAN ACTUALLY BE HAPPY AND RELAXED -- yeah, even while you're a student!

TotallyStressedOut.com
The stress management site for students

THE BACK of the BOOK

Corrections to this book can be found at

Coolmath.com/oops
(Hopefully, there won't be any!)

If you find a mistake in this book you can also go here to report it to me.
Of course, if you do find a mistake, then that was the part I let my cat write.

pg 36: $3 \cdot x \cdot x \cdot x$, 48, 1875
pg 37: $8a^3bc^5$
pg 38: y^7
pg 39: x^{149}
pg 40: $6x^9 y^{10} w^{13}$
pg 41: y^5
pg 42: $\dfrac{1}{x^3}$

pg 44: $\dfrac{3x^2}{11wz^8}$, $\dfrac{1}{2w^{10}z^2w^8}$

pg 46: w^9
pg 47: $2w^{44}x^{18}z^{30}$
pg 49: $\dfrac{1}{81}$, $\dfrac{1}{4}$, 25
pg 50: $\dfrac{2a^5 d^4}{5b^3 c e^6}$
pg 52: $5x^{20}w^{12}z^{11}$
$\dfrac{3}{13w^4 z^{10} x^{10}}$

pg 53: $\dfrac{-x^{29} z^4}{6w^{10}}$

pg 54: $x^2 x^4$
$= xxxxxx = x^6$

pg 55: $\dfrac{xx}{xxxxxxxx}$
$= \dfrac{1}{xxxxxx} = \dfrac{1}{x^6}$

pg 56: $\dfrac{x^3}{6}$

pg 57: $\dfrac{6}{x^4}$

pg 58: $(wz)(wz)(wz)$
$= wwwzzz = w^3 z^3$

pg 59: $16x^2 y^{10} z^6$

pg 62: $\left(\dfrac{w}{z}\right)\left(\dfrac{w}{z}\right)\left(\dfrac{w}{z}\right)$
$= \dfrac{www}{zzz} = \dfrac{w^3}{z^3}$

pg 63: $\dfrac{81 a^{20} b^8}{16 c^4}$

$\dfrac{512 x^9 w^6 z^{18}}{27}$

pg 65: 3, $\sqrt{37}$, can't do yet
pg 68: can't do, 1, 0, -4, 3, 9, can't do
pg 70: 3
pg 71: 6, can't do, 240
pg 72: $\dfrac{1}{10}$, 5, 15
pg 75: $3\sqrt{5}$
pg 76: $15\sqrt{7}$, $3\sqrt[3]{2}$
pg 79: $\sqrt{5}$
pg 80: 2
pg 82: $\dfrac{2\sqrt{15}}{5}$
pg 84: $\dfrac{6+3\sqrt{6}}{-2} = \dfrac{-6-3\sqrt{6}}{2}$
pg 87: 243

pg 88: $\dfrac{a^2 b^4}{4}$, $\dfrac{27 a^3}{b^6}$

pg 95: $-3, 6$

pg 99: $2, 5, 1$

pg 102: $9x - 2w + 6z$

pg 103: $10x^2 + 5x + 4$

$5a^2 b + 7ab + 3b^2 - 6a^2 + 4$

pg 104: $2x^2 - 11x + 13$, 2

pg 105: $-2x^2 + 2xy + 4y^2$

pg 106: $12x^6 + 18x^4$

pg 107:
$20x^8 - 30x^5 + 10x^4 + 10x^3$
$4x^2 w^6 - 4x^4 w^5 + 24 x^3 w^7 - 4x^2 w^5 + 12 x^6 w^{13}$

pg 109: $12x^2 - 6x - 21$

pg 110: $10w^2 - 57wz - 18z^2$

pg 111: $4x^3 + 10x^2 + 18$

pg 112: $10,994$

pg 115: $2x(x-2)$, $7x(1+2x)$

pg 117:
$5ab^3 (3ab - 1 + 4a^2 + 2a^4 b^4)$
$2x^2 y^2 (3x^2 y + 1 - 4x^3 y^4)$

pg 121: $x^2 - 3x - 10$
$x^2 + 6x + 9$
$x^2 - 13x + 42$
$x^2 + 9x + 8$

pg 124: $(x+4)(x-5)$
$(a+3)(a-8)$

pg 125: $(y+3)(y+5)$
$(x+9)(x-10)$

pg 126: $(y-1)(y+11)$

pg 127: $(x-21)(x+1)$
$(y-2)(y+14)$

pg 128: $(a+4b)(a-12b)$

pg 133: $(3x-7)(x+1)$
$(x+7)(5x+1)$

pg 135: $(x-2)(3x+4)$

pg 137: $(3x-5)(4x+1)$

pg 141: $(3x-2)(2x+5)$

pg 143: possibilities are:
$(x \quad 2)(7x \quad 5)$ no
$(x \quad 1)(7x \quad 10)$ no
$(7x \quad 1)(x \quad 10)$ no
$(7x+2)(x-5)$
gives -10 no!

pg 145: $(y-4)(y+4)$
$(2x-9)(2x+9)$

pg 147: $(5x-1)(25x^2 + 5x + 1)$

pg 148: $(2a+b)(4a^2 - 2ab + b^2)$

pg 149: $w(5+3x)$
$y^2 (5+3x)$
$k^3 (5+3x)$
(blob)$(5+3x)$
$(w+2)(5+3x)$

pg 150: $(x-6)(3x^3 + 4)$
$(w^2 + 1)(9y - 4x)$

pg 151: $(x-6)(3x^3 + 4)$

THE BACK OF THE BOOK

pg 152: $(\omega^2+1)(9y-4x)$

pg 158: $1 - \dfrac{5\omega}{y^2} + \dfrac{3}{2y} - \dfrac{7}{4\omega y^2}$

pg 160: $26,307$

pg 166: $5x^2 - 4x + 6$

pg 169: $4x^2 + 2x + 1$

pg 172: $x^2 + x + 4 + \dfrac{6}{x-3}$

pg 180: $x = 9$

pg 182: $x = 13/5$

pg 184: $x = 24$

pg 186: $x = 6$

pg 188: $x = -5$

pg 189: $x = 3$

pg 191: $x = 5/11$

pg 194: $x = 9/4$

pg 195: $x = 54/5$

pg 197: $x = 7/100$

pg 198: $x = 989/600$

pg 199: $x = 47/331$
$x = 300/1531$

pg 201:

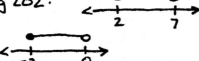

pg 202:

pg 203:

pg 207: $[2,5)$, $[0,7]$, $(-6,4)$, $(-10,0)$

pg 208: $[2,\infty)$, $(-\infty,4)$, $(0,\infty)$, $(-\infty,-3]$

pg 209: $(-\infty,-5] \cup (0,\infty)$
$(-\infty,3] \cup [10,\infty)$
$(-\infty,0) \cup (2,\infty)$

pg 213: $x \leq 2$, $(-\infty, 2]$
$x > 7$, $(7, \infty)$

pg 216: $x < -15$, $(-\infty,-5)$

pg 217: $x > -3$, $(-3, \infty)$
$x \leq -4$, $(-\infty, -4]$

pg 220: $-2 < x \leq 3$, $(-2, 3]$
$2/5 \leq x \leq 9/5$, $[2/5, 9/5]$

pg 235:

pg 240: slope $= 7/5$

pg 242: $m = 7/5$

pg 244:

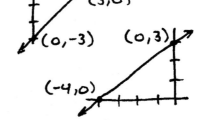

pg 246:

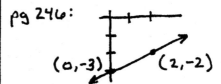

pg 248: slope = 0
pg 249: slope is undefined
pg 251:

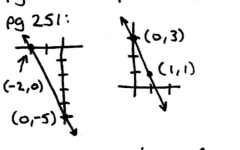

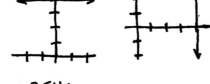

pg 254: $y = -\frac{1}{4}x$

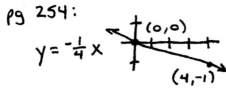

pg 256: m = 3
pg 257: m = $-\frac{7}{2}$
pg 259: y = 3x + 12
or −3x + y = 12

pg 260: $y = \frac{2}{5}x - \frac{42}{5}$
or 2x − 5y = 42
pg 263: $y = -\frac{4}{3}x - \frac{1}{3}$
or 4x + 3y = −1
pg 266: m = $-\frac{3}{5}$
$y = -\frac{3}{5}x - \frac{7}{5}$ or 3x + 5y = −7
pg 270: m = $-\frac{1}{3}$
$y = -\frac{1}{3}x + \frac{4}{3}$ or x + 3y = 4
pg 274:

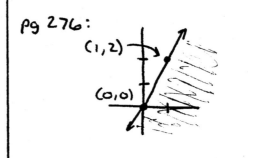

pg 276:

Remember that the answers to life's questions are not in the back of the book!

Are you already in credit card trouble?
Is your FICO score the pits?
Uh... FICO who?
Do you want to learn about this stuff?

Do you want to learn how to be SMART & RICH?

financeFREAK.com

A fool and his money are soon parted.
Don't be a fool... Be a FREAK!

ARE YOU TOTALLY STRESSED OUT?

You don't have to feel out of control. You don't have to feel nervous. You don't have to feel tired and foggy all the time. Believe me, I've been there myself. I totally remember what it was like to be a student -- and I was a student for a LONG time! Since then, I've been a college teacher so I'm around students all the time - most of them stressed out. Over the years, I've been teaching my students how to de-stress and how to deal with stress... I finally decided to make a stress management site specially designed FOR students -- and anyone else who feels stressed out.

So, settle down and KNOW that you CAN lower your stress! You really ARE in control of what's going on in your world!
YOU CAN ACTUALLY BE HAPPY AND RELAXED -- yeah, even while you're a student!

TotallyStressedOut.com
The stress management site for students